Locke: A Very Short Introduction

VERY SHORT INTRODUCTIONS are for anyone wanting a stimulating and accessible way into a new subject. They are written by experts, and have been translated into more than 45 different languages.

The series began in 1995, and now covers a wide variety of topics in every discipline. The VSI library now contains over 500 volumes—a Very Short Introduction to everything from Psychology and Philosophy of Science to American History and Relativity—and continues to grow in every subject area.

Titles in the series include the following:

AFRICAN HISTORY John Parker and
    Richard Rathbone
AMERICAN HISTORY Paul S. Boyer
AMERICAN LEGAL HISTORY
    G. Edward White
AMERICAN POLITICAL PARTIES
    AND ELECTIONS L. Sandy Maisel
AMERICAN POLITICS
    Richard M. Valelly
AMERICAN SLAVERY
    Heather Andrea Williams
ANARCHISM Colin Ward
ANCIENT EGYPT Ian Shaw
ANCIENT GREECE Paul Cartledge
ANCIENT PHILOSOPHY Julia Annas
ANCIENT WARFARE Harry Sidebottom
ANGLICANISM Mark Chapman
THE ANGLO-SAXON AGE John Blair
ANIMAL RIGHTS David DeGrazia
ARCHAEOLOGY Paul Bahn
ARISTOTLE Jonathan Barnes
ART HISTORY Dana Arnold
ART THEORY Cynthia Freeland
ATHEISM Julian Baggini
THE ATMOSPHERE Paul I. Palmer
AUGUSTINE Henry Chadwick
BACTERIA Sebastian G. B. Amyes
BEAUTY Roger Scruton
THE BIBLE John Riches
BLACK HOLES Katherine Blundell
BLOOD Chris Cooper
THE BRAIN Michael O'Shea
THE BRICS Andrew F. Cooper
BRITISH POLITICS Anthony Wright

BUDDHA Michael Carrithers
BUDDHISM Damien Keown
BUDDHIST ETHICS Damien Keown
CAPITALISM James Fulcher
CATHOLICISM Gerald O'Collins
THE CELTS Barry Cunliffe
CHOICE THEORY Michael Allingham
CHRISTIANITY Linda Woodhead
CIRCADIAN RHYTHMS Russell Foster
    and Leon Kreitzman
CITIZENSHIP Richard Bellamy
CLASSICAL MYTHOLOGY
    Helen Morales
CLASSICS Mary Beard and
    John Henderson
CLIMATE CHANGE Mark Maslin
THE COLD WAR Robert McMahon
COMMUNISM Leslie Holmes
CONSCIOUSNESS Susan Blackmore
CONTEMPORARY ART
    Julian Stallabrass
COSMOLOGY Peter Coles
THE CRUSADES Christopher Tyerman
DADA AND SURREALISM
    David Hopkins
DARWIN Jonathan Howard
THE DEAD SEA SCROLLS
    Timothy Lim
DECOLONIZATION Dane Kennedy
DEMOCRACY Bernard Crick
DESIGN John Heskett
DREAMING J. Allan Hobson
DRUGS Les Iversen
THE EARTH Martin Redfern

John Dunn

LOCKE

A Very Short Introduction

OXFORD
UNIVERSITY PRESS

Great Clarendon Street, Oxford OX2 6DP

Oxford University Press is a department of the University of Oxford.
It furthers the University's objective of excellence in research, scholarship,
and education by publishing worldwide in

Oxford New York

Auckland Bangkok Buenos Aires Cape Town Chennai
Dar es Salaam Delhi Hong Kong Istanbul Karachi Kolkata
Kuala Lumpur Madrid Melbourne Mexico City Mumbai Nairobi
São Paulo Shanghai Taipei Tokyo Toronto

Oxford is a registered trade mark of Oxford University Press
in the UK and in certain other countries

Published in the United States
by Oxford University Press Inc., New York

British Library Cataloguing in Publication Data
Data available

Library of Congress Cataloging in Publication Data
Data available

ISBN 978-0-19-280394-8

Typeset by RefineCatch Ltd, Bungay, Suffolk

Printed and bound by
CPI Group (UK) Ltd, Croydon, CR0 4YY

To the memory of Peter Laslett

New preface

Since the first version of this book was published in Oxford University Press's 'Past Masters' series in 1984, I have been made to think again about very many aspects of Locke's life by the promptings of a succession of generous friends and fellow scholars: Quentin Skinner, John Kenyon, Judith Shklar, Istvan Hont, Pasquale Pasquino, Bernard Manin, Ole Grell, Avishai Margalit, Ian Harris, John Marshall, Sudipta Kaviraj, Sunil Khilnani, Gary McDowell, and most recently Ian Shapiro. I have also had the singular privilege of working on the Board of the Clarendon Edition of Locke's *Collected Works* under two general editors, John Yolton and Sandy Stewart. These experiences have altered greatly the way in which I see the significance of many aspects of Locke's achievements. But they have done nothing to modify the way in which I saw the man himself whilst I was writing this book, or to change the judgements about the contents of his works which it expresses. Over this time, I have learnt a great deal and forgotten a truly awesome amount. But I still stand by the picture which the book tries to convey, and have therefore chosen not to modify the prose in which it is written, even where (as with the use of the term 'man' to cover all human beings) I would probably phrase some points differently today.

It is a pleasure to take the opportunity of this new guise to thank those who, since 1983, have converted a somewhat casually selected work of apprenticeship into a lifetime's intellectual debt, and the many polished and congenial editors at Oxford University Press with whom I have worked on Locke matters, notably Angela Blackburn and Peter Momtchiloff, and now Emma Simmons. I would like to dedicate this new version to the memory of Peter Laslett, my incomparable and sadly missed graduate supervisor, who did more by his zest, insight, and inexhaustible energy to keep Locke's memory alive and make it possible for others to judge his real purposes than anyone has done for well over a century.

Preface

Locke addressed his intellectual life as a whole to two huge questions. How is it that human beings can know anything? And how should they try to live? He began his career as a university teacher and ended it as very much a man of the world. In its course he thought, and thought hard, about a bewildering range of issues, from the prospects for English foreign trade and the economic consequences of the state of the English coinage to the politics of revolution in the 1680s, the interpretation of St Paul's *Epistles*, and the cultivation of fruit trees. Because his interests were so broad, and because he pursued them with such intelligence and energy, he left behind him a large and impressive body of writings. In a brief work it would be impossible to do justice to the range of his ideas, let alone to assess their originality and unravel their intricate contribution to the intellectual history of the next two centuries. Accordingly, I shall not attempt to assess in any detail the contribution which he made to the various branches of modern thought: economics, theology, political theory, scriptural interpretation, ethics, anthropology, the theory of knowledge, education, and so on. (In particular, I shall not set out a systematic exposition and criticism of his theory of knowledge as a classical moment in the history of British empiricism. To do so would distort his own approach; and it would also, in my view, do little to illuminate questions of current interest.) Instead, I shall focus on the shape of Locke's intellectual life as a whole and attempt to explain how he saw the relation between the two huge and unwieldy questions which he addressed with such courage and tenacity over so many years.

During the last two decades of his life, from 1683 until his death in 1704, it was the question of how men can know to which he devoted his keenest intellectual energies. His answer to it, however poorly understood, marked the mind of Europe for generations. Philosophers today disagree sharply on the merits of this answer. Some see it as a more or less mistaken response to a legitimate and important question. Others regard the question itself as confused and the demand for a comprehensive explanation of the scope and limits of men's cognitive powers as both absurd and impossible to satisfy. Still others see Locke's approach as fundamentally correct, whatever errors he may have made in working it out. It would be presumptuous here to pretend to adjudicate this disagreement. But it is essential to try to show what made Locke himself so eager to construct a theory of knowledge.

It was the second question, the question of how men should try to live, from which his thinking began. By the end of his life he was confident that he had largely answered the question of how men can know – at least in so far as its answer lay within the reach of human powers. But he was far less confident of his ability, on the basis of human powers alone, to show men how they should try to live. Initially he had hoped that an explanation of men's power to know would show them *why* they should try to live as he supposed they should. But the theory of knowledge which he constructed proved to show nothing of the kind. In consequence his theory of practical reason (of what men have good reason to do) was from his own point of view a disastrous failure. Unlike his theory of knowledge, it offers scarcely even the core of a view which we might ourselves hold. Some philosophers today do not regard the question of how men should try to live as a philosophical question at all; and more would not regard it as very clearly expressed. For these or other reasons, Locke's enterprise may well have been doomed from the start; but it remains profoundly instructive. The greatness of a thinker is not always best measured by the confidence and clarity of his intellectual solutions. Sometimes it can be shown at least as dramatically by the resonance of his failures.

What Locke hoped to show men was that a rational understanding of man's place in nature required them to live like Christians. But what he in fact showed was that a rational understanding of their place in nature did not, and does not, *require* men to live in any particular fashion. Worse still, the close relation between conceptions of how to live and the history of particular languages and cultures places all men's lives at the mercy of history. Even if there were a God who had designed the order of nature as a whole for men to live well within it, they could not draw their conceptions of how to live directly from this order through the exercise of their reason alone. Instead they must fashion their values for themselves as best they can out of the more or less seductive or menacing suggestions of others and by their own powers of reflection.

Our views today about how we can know still owe something to Locke. It remains an open question whether they would benefit from, for example, owing more to a better understood Locke or from purging what they still owe to a not very well understood Locke. Our views today about how we should try to live owe little directly to Locke's own beliefs. But it may well be that we have still not taken the measure of his failure. On the whole, Locke is discussed by historians and philosophers today as an optimistic thinker whose optimism was founded on understanding not very well what we ourselves understand altogether better. The case which I wish to put in this book is very different. It is that we should see Locke instead as a tragic thinker, who understood in advance some of the deep contradictions in the modern conception of human reason, and so saw rather clearly some of the tragedy of our own lives which we still see very dimly indeed.

Contents

Abbreviations

The following abbreviations are used in references to Locke's works:

E   *An Essay concerning Human Understanding*, ed. Peter H. Nidditch (Clarendon Press, 1975).

EA   *Draft A of Locke's Essay concerning Human Understanding*, ed. Peter H. Nidditch (Department of Philosophy, University of Sheffield, 1980).

G   *Two Tracts on Government*, ed. Philip Abrams (Cambridge University Press, 1967).

LC   *The Correspondence of John Locke*, ed. E. S. de Beer, 8 vols. (Clarendon Press, 1976).

LN   *Essays on the Law of Nature*, ed. W. von Leyden (Clarendon Press, 1954).

LT   *Epistola de Tolerantia and A Letter on Toleration*, ed. R. Klibansky and J. W. Gough (Clarendon Press, 1968).

M   *An Examination of P. Malebranche's Opinion of Seeing All Things in God, Works*, 7th edn. (London, 1768), iv.

R   *The Reasonableness of Christianity as delivered in the Scriptures, Works*, 7th edn. (London, 1768), iii.

T   *Two Treatises of Government*, ed. Peter Laslett, 2nd edn. (Cambridge University Press, 1967).

V   *Venditio*, printed in J. Dunn, 'Justice and the Interpretation of Locke's Political Theory', *Political Studies*, 16/1 (Feb. 1968), 84–7.

W   *The Works of John Locke*, 7th edn., 4 vols. (London, 1768).

Important manuscript texts by Locke are cited from:

D   John Dunn, *The Political Thought of John Locke* (Cambridge University Press, 1969).

FB   H. R. Fox Bourne, *The Life of John Locke*, 2 vols. (London, 1876).

List of illustrations

The publisher and the author apologize for any errors or omissions in the above list. If contacted they will be pleased to rectify these at the earliest opportunity.

Acknowledgements

I am deeply grateful to Michael Ayers for his generosity in lending me in manuscript a large portion of his major study of Locke's philosophy and for the pleasure and excitement which I have derived over many years from his remarkable knowledge and understanding of Locke's works. For Oxford University Press, Henry Hardy, Keith Thomas, and Alan Ryan have given me extremely helpful advice in preparing the text and have shown me throughout far more patience than I deserved. I am greatly indebted, as so often before, to many friends who have at different stages and for different reasons read drafts of part or all of it. For their encouragement, help, and criticism I should particularly like to thank Cynthia Farrar, Michael Ignatieff, Takashi Kato, Jonathan Lear, and Quentin Skinner.

Chapter 1
Life

John Locke was born in a Somerset village in the summer of 1632. He died in the country house of his friends the Mashams, at Oates in Essex, late in October 1704. Until his mid-thirties he lived what was, at least in its externals, a rather unexciting life. But for more than three decades – from the year 1667 – he was closely involved with the vagaries of English national politics. In his late fifties, for the first time and quite suddenly, he became a very famous man. From then on almost any of his correspondents might have described him without irony, with Lady Mary Calverley, as simply 'the greatest man in the world' (LC IV 105). When at last it did come, fame came to him as a philosopher, from the publication of his writings and especially, in the year 1689, of the great *Essay concerning Human Understanding*. It is this fame which has persisted, without interruption, until today.

By the time that Locke was 40 he had in most ways grown very far away from his Somerset origins; and the real social distance between him and the rest of his family must have widened fairly steadily for the rest of his life. But in some fundamental respects, what he owed (for better or worse) to his parental upbringing remained the centre of his feelings and attitudes until the day he died. It is unusual in the case of a man or woman of the 17th century to be able to assess continuities of this kind with any confidence. But one of the peculiarities of Locke's temperament was his extreme reluctance to throw away any papers on which he had written. Since, by great good fortune, most of those which remained at his death have come down to us, we do in fact know more about him than we do about all but a handful of his contemporaries or predecessors. What this mass of manuscripts makes clear is that throughout adulthood Locke sustained a deeply Puritan pattern of sentiment, a pattern which places a sense of duty at the centre of the individual life. He was not in any way a morose and joyless person. But he did impose very fierce demands, upon himself as much as on others; and he was extremely moralistic in his reactions when these demands were not met. There was nothing Puritan about most of the philosophical views which won him immortality; and many of them would have shocked any Puritan alive in 1632. But the personal identity which gave his thought as a whole its integrity and human depth was that of a deeply Puritan self.

Locke's father and mother each came from Puritan trading families, clothiers on the father's side and tanners on the mother's. His father earned a not very impressive living as an attorney and clerk to the

1. **Locke's birthplace at Wrington, Somerset. Not a hovel, even seen two centuries later, but very far from grand.**

Justices of the Peace in Somerset. In addition he owned some land; not enough in itself to enable either him or his son to live the life of a gentleman, but enough to lead the son in later years to style himself as such on the title-page of his greatest work. In itself this background did not guarantee Locke much of a future. But if his immediate family was parochial in its interests and somewhat ineffectual in its worldly pursuits, it did have more powerful and successful acquaintances. The most important of these was Alexander Popham. Like Locke's father, Popham had fought as an officer in the Parliamentary cavalry in Somerset in the early stages of the Civil War; and he went on to be a West Country Member of Parliament and a prominent figure in national politics. In 1647, as Member of Parliament for Bath, he was in a position to offer his attorney and brother officer the opportunity to send the latter's elder son to Westminster school. In later years Locke's father continued to hope for patronage from his influential political allies. But except perhaps for his son's crucial passage from Westminster school to Christ Church, Oxford, where a powerful patron appears once again to have been indispensable, his hopes seem always to have been disappointed. But if he left little impact upon a wider world, it is clear enough that this austere and, in later life, somewhat embittered man left a deep impress upon his brilliant son: an independence of spirit and force of self-discipline which were to mould Locke's entire life.

It is easiest to see the shape of this life in terms of three large movements, each of which carried Locke further away from his Somerset origins. The first move, to Westminster and then to Christ Church, marked the furthest stretch of his family's own resources and reasonable expectations. It carried him within easy reach of a clerical career, either inside or outside the university, a career which, with only moderate fortune and prudence, might fully match his intellectual abilities. ('A man of parts,' wrote his cousin John Strachey, 'let him study but complyance, hee need want noe preferment' (LC I 215).) But even as a young man with very few prospects, Locke clearly did not find compliance agreeable; and he

3

seems never to have been attracted by the idea of a clerical career. A second possibility, less conventional and narrower but also more congenial, was to become a doctor. This was a possibility which Locke in fact pursued with some vigour, studying medicine systematically over several decades and offering extensive medical advice to friends and acquaintances. He worked closely with one of the great physicians of the 17th century, Dr Thomas Sydenham, a pioneer in the treatment of infectious diseases. Sydenham's approach to the study of illness was unusually self-conscious and systematic, and Locke's own conception of how men come to know about the natural world may well have been influenced by this collaboration. Fittingly, also, it was his medical interests, not his expertise as a philosopher or theologian, which gave him the great opportunity of his life.

The second movement came in 1666. In that year, through another medical friend, David Thomas, Locke met for the first time Lord Ashley, later the first Earl of Shaftesbury, a leading political figure at the court of Charles II. The occasion for the meeting was casual enough – a visit by Ashley to Oxford to drink the spa waters of Astrop. But its consequences, for Locke at least, were momentous. Within a year of this first meeting he had joined Ashley's household in London. A year later, in 1668, his patron underwent under Locke's supervision a major operation, for a suppurating cyst on the liver, and against all the odds the operation proved successful. For the next 14 years he 'studied complyance' with Shaftesbury's whims and shared his master's turbulent fortunes. The move from the placid, if sometimes ill-tempered, backwater of Restoration Oxford to the seething life of Shaftesbury's household was a drastic one. Not that Locke himself ever voluntarily abandoned his position at Oxford (he was in fact expelled from it on government instructions after fleeing into exile in 1683); but the weight of his energies and hopes and fears, for the remainder of his life, rested elsewhere. From this time on, his personal fortunes rose and fell with those of his master and, after Shaftesbury's death in 1683, with those of the broad political grouping he had led.

2. Thomas Sydenham, medical pioneer and inspiration for much of Locke's early conception of medical and scientific method.

In the years between 1667 and 1683 Shaftesbury was at different stages the most powerful political figure at Charles II's court and the leader of a national political opposition to that court which in the end threatened and perhaps planned a revolution to overthrow it. Both his triumphs and his failures marked Locke's imagination deeply. It was Shaftesbury who taught him to understand the economic responsibilities of the English State in its domestic market and in foreign commerce, who taught him to see the conditions and possibilities for economic prosperity as a central preoccupation for statecraft and a fundamental consideration in assessing any society's merits. If Locke's intellectual energies were in the end harnessed to any great degree by the cruel but vigorous dynamism of the English economy of his day, it was Shaftesbury who caused them to be so. There is a direct line of continuity between Locke's service on the Council of Trade during Shaftesbury's Chancellorship in 1672 and his service on William's Board of Trade in the 1690s, and an equally direct line between the economic understanding set out in his first economic writing in 1668 and the major works on regulating the rate of interest and on restoring the coinage which he wrote to advise William's government. Equally direct in terms of content, though not perhaps of motivation, is the link between Shaftesbury's steady commitment to toleration for Dissenters in the face of Restoration Anglicanism and Locke's spirited public and private campaign for toleration and freedom of the Press in the last two decades of his life. Equally clear is the tie between Shaftesbury's somewhat belated insistence, in the course of the so-called Exclusion crisis (the struggle to exclude Charles II's Catholic brother, James Duke of York, from the succession to the throne), on the representative basis of political legitimacy and Locke's great defence, in the *Two Treatises of Government*, of the rights to be governed only with consent and to resist unjust power.

The extent of this impact was, no doubt, largely a consequence simply of the range of experience which Shaftesbury's service opened up to Locke, the quite new practical vision of the social and political world with which it presented him. But it is clear, too, that it was a deeply personal impact. In the course of his life Locke had many close friends and very many more friends who, if less close, were also men and women of great power or wealth or very high intelligence: political grandees like Pembroke and Somers, scientists like Robert Boyle and Isaac Newton, theologians like Limborch. However much he liked and respected Locke as a man, Shaftesbury was, of course, very much master as well as friend. But

3. Locke's great patron, first Earl of Shaftesbury, leading minister, and later bitter opponent, of Charles II.

lop-sided though their friendship plainly was, it did not lack emotional energy; and over those 16 years it is clear that his great patron made Locke into a very different man.

They make a strange pair, these two figures between whom Locke's adult life was moulded: the awkward, repressed failure of a father and the glittering, untrustworthy, endlessly fascinating courtier who at the close of his life failed far more spectacularly. Strange –

but in some ways singularly propitious. For each served admirably to offset the deficiencies in imagination of the other: the worried, ineradicable scruple of the first and the force, recklessness, and irresponsibility of the second. From the tension between the two – and after the death of each – came the extraordinary intellectual framework of Locke's philosophy.

This third movement, the commitment to philosophical understanding, was, of course, far less obvious to the outsider and more gradual than either the shift to Westminster and Oxford or the entry into Shaftesbury's service. Locke's concern with philosophical questions of political authority and toleration, of ethics and the theory of knowledge, went back at least to the late 1650s. Indeed there is no reason to suppose that he would not have thought and written at length about philosophy if he had in fact taken holy orders, had never encountered Shaftesbury, and had remained an Oxford don for the rest of his life. Nor did he ever succeed, until he was a very old and sick man, in extricating himself from the political and public responsibilities in which Shaftesbury's service had initially involved him. But if philosophy and politics continued to compete for his energies and attention from 1667 until shortly before his death, the balance between the two was struck very differently at different stages of his life.

Up until the year 1667, during the 15 years which he spent at Oxford as a Student at Christ Church, Locke's philosophical writing was confined essentially to two major pieces of work. The first of these was a pair of essays on the demerits of claims to religious toleration, one in English and one in Latin, written in 1660 and 1661 and unpublished until the 20th century, the *Two Tracts on Government*. The second was a set of Latin lectures on the law of nature, delivered by him in 1664 as Censor of Moral Philosophy at Christ Church and also unpublished until the 20th century, the *Essays on the Law of Nature*. The questions of the scope and limits of religious liberty and of how men ought to live remained central to Locke's thinking in later decades. But these first two pieces of

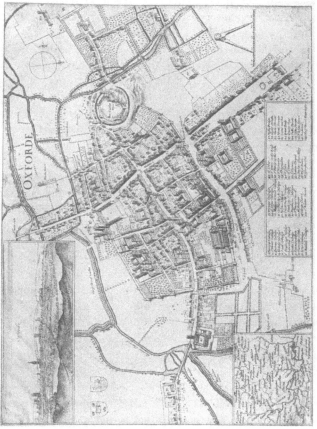

4. Oxford in mid-century: the problem of religious toleration shrunk to the scale of an inglorious College squabble (surplices in the College sewer).

writing lacked the breadth and urgency of his mature works; and they showed a very different political attitude. The most important intellectual opportunity which Oxford offered him in these years was not the chance to begin to work out and express what we should now think of as philosophical opinions, but rather the chance to participate in the chemical and medical researches of Boyle, Hooke, Lower and Sydenham. From these men Locke learnt the value of sustained and disciplined observation, of humility, patience, and diligence in man's attempt to grasp the secrets of nature. As Sydenham put it in 1669, in a manuscript written in Locke's own hand:

> True knowledge grew first in the world by experience and rational observation, but proud man, not content with the knowledge he was capable of, and which was useful to him, would needs penetrate into the hidden causes of things, lay down principles, and establish maxims to himself about the operations of nature, and thus vainly expect that nature, or in truth God should proceed according to those laws which his maxims had prescribed to him.

It was this background of practical scientific enquiry which Locke brought to bear on his reading of the two great Continental philosophers of the early scientific revolution, René Descartes and Pierre Gassendi, whose views affected him deeply in the late 1660s. Of the two, Locke's mature views were in many ways considerably closer to those of Gassendi. But, as he told Lady Masham, it was those of Descartes which first strongly attracted him to philosophy, to the attempt to understand very precisely and systematically what knowledge man 'was capable of'. The *Essay concerning Human Understanding* itself was, as he said in his *Epistle to the Reader*, an attempt 'to examine our own abilities, and see what objects our understandings were or were not fitted to deal with'. Most of the *Essay* was not in fact written until the late 1680s. But there exist extended drafts of many of the main arguments which were written as early as the year 1671. Besides these first sketches of the *Essay*,

Locke also wrote other important works in this period: in 1668 a lengthy manuscript on the futility of governmental efforts to regulate the rate of interest, and in 1667 an essay on toleration, fully in the spirit of Shaftesbury's policies on the subject and decisively reversing his own more authoritarian views of the early 1660s. On the whole, however, his time in these years was too taken up with administrative work in Shaftesbury's public or private concerns, as colonial proprietor, great landowner and Minister of the Crown, to leave him the leisure for sustained philosophical work. By 1675 Shaftesbury was firmly in opposition to the King's government under Danby, and Locke himself was in very poor health. For the next three and a half years, a time of considerable danger for Shaftesbury, Locke travelled in France, for much of it in the rather trying company of Caleb Banks, the son of one of Shaftesbury's richest political associates. In the course of his travels he met many French doctors, scientists and theologians and made close friends with several of them. He also translated some of the moral essays of the Jansenist Pierre Nicole. But he does not appear to have worked on any original writings of his own.

At the end of April 1679, however, he returned to London. The next four years, up to the late summer of 1683 when he fled to Rotterdam, are a time of some obscurity in his life. His patron Shaftesbury had already lost his political influence at court by the time of Locke's departure to France in 1675. Even at this point Locke's services to him 'in his library and closet' were no longer confined to the 'business of a Minister of State'. He may well, for example, have drafted the 1675 pamphlet, *A Letter from a Person of Quality to his Friend in the Country*, in which Shaftesbury's opposition programme was set out; a pamphlet which earned the distinction of being burnt by the public hangman. By 1679 Shaftesbury's opposition to the policies of Charles II's government had sharpened. In the course of the next four years, during the Exclusion crisis, he organized and led a national political movement against the Crown, aimed at strengthening the constitutional restraints on royal authority, protecting the rights of the elected House of Commons and excluding Charles II's Catholic brother James from the succession to the throne. It was a bitter and dangerous struggle in which the line between exercising legally recognized political rights and committing high treason was always difficult to draw. But there was no doubt at all of Charles's eagerness to draw it at the earliest possible stage. By 1682, if not before, Shaftesbury himself and Locke, Algernon Sidney, Lord William Russell, and the Earl of Essex were all gambling with their lives. In the event Shaftesbury, at least, contrived to escape to the Netherlands, where he promptly died. But in June 1683, after the failure of the Rye House Plot to kidnap Charles and James on their return from Newmarket races, Sidney, Russell, and Essex were all arrested. Essex subsequently committed suicide in the Tower of London, while Russell and Sidney met their deaths on the scaffold. Amongst the charges against Sidney at his trial was the authorship of seditious manuscripts. The latter included a lengthy attack on Sir Robert Filmer's ultra-royalist tract *Patriarcha*, an attack which was published posthumously, following Sidney's execution, as his *Discourses on Government*. Locke too was certainly under close governmental observation during the late summer of 1683, though he was scarcely a figure of the political importance of Essex, Russell, or even Sidney. But he too, it now seems clear, must have had in his possession at that time an extremely seditious manuscript, the *Two Treatises of Government*, which likewise attacked the political theories of Filmer and which roundly endorsed the people's right of revolution against even a legitimate monarch where that monarch had grossly abused his powers. As it turned out, Locke managed to slip away into exile in Holland by September 1683; and, although his Christ Church Studentship was withdrawn from him on royal command the next year, and the British government made unsuccessful attempts in 1685 to have him extradited, along with other Whig exiles, he was in much less danger from then on.

Exactly when and why he settled down to write the *Two Treatises* is still unclear and it is likely to remain so. Sedition was a hazardous business in 17th-century England; and the *Two Treatises of Government*, written in the circumstances of the Exclusion crisis, was an intensely seditious work. At least from 1683 on Locke showed himself to be a markedly cautious and secretive person. But we do know one or two interesting details about what he was doing in these years. In 1680, for example, he spent a considerable amount of time at Oakley, the country house of his friend James Tyrrell, who himself in 1681 published an attack on the political theory of Filmer, *Patriarcha non Monarcha*. Between 1680 and perhaps 1682 Tyrrell and Locke worked together on a lengthy (and still unpublished) manuscript work, defending the principles of toleration against a leading Anglican apologist, Edward Stillingfleet. It was to Tyrrell, amongst others, as a government spy reported, that Locke entrusted 'several handbaskets of papers' while preparing for his departure from Oxford in July 1683. For Shaftesbury's political followers in those years, the defence of the political and religious rights of the Dissenters and the criticism of the most vehement English theorist of royal absolutism were both tasks of great urgency.

When he went into exile late in the summer of 1683 Locke had already passed the age of 50 and had published nothing of his own which was of the least consequence. The only major work of his own which we may be certain had been written for publication, the *Two Treatises of Government*, was for the moment more a source of hazard than a ground for self-congratulation. On the other hand, exile, however disagreeable and even dangerous in some ways, did present certain opportunities. For one thing, Locke made many friends, some of them very close, amongst the English merchant community and Dutch theologians and, after the revocation of the Edict of Nantes in 1685, amongst French Protestant refugees. For another, he had the time to think and write systematically and at length, without the immediate distractions of politics. He might not be in good health and his worldly prospects might be unenticing, but at least he had the chance to muster his powers and leave something substantial to posterity. It was during these years that he wrote both the *Essay concerning Human Understanding* and the *Letter on Toleration.*

In 1688 his worldly prospects improved sharply, with the landing of the Protestant William of Orange in England and the flight of the Roman Catholic King James II. Early the next year Locke returned to England and in the course of it his three greatest works were printed. Two appeared anonymously, the *Letter on Toleration* first in Latin in Holland in April and then in English in London in October, and the *Two Treatises of Government* in London at the end of the year. But one, the *Essay concerning Human Understanding,* was issued in mid-December in a fine folio volume and with his own name firmly on the title-page. It was a remarkable publishing debut.

In the 15 years which remained to him before his death in 1704 his commitments remained as diverse as ever. Some were political in the narrowest sense: the consolidation of William's constitutional and political position, the reorganization of the English coinage, the establishment of an effective credit system for the English State through the new Bank of England, and the development of institutions through which the government could exercise more effectively its responsibilities for the prosperity of English foreign trade. In each of these Locke himself was actively engaged, in the last three as a trusted intellectual adviser to the country's leading statesmen and over foreign trade as a lavishly rewarded public official on the new Board of Trade. Each of these preoccupations represented, in some measure, a fulfilment of Shaftesbury's programme of the late 1660s and early 1670s, a programme of highly self-conscious commercial imperialism in a narrowly English interest. In the legal and political arrangements of the Revolution settlement Locke played a more discreet and a considerably less influential role. It seems likely, too, that on the central issue of constitutional reform and the increase in the political power of an elected legislature, the outcome was much further from his wishes than it was in the case of monetary, fiscal, or economic policy. More importantly perhaps, it is also clear that the political character of the Revolution settlement engaged his feelings and beliefs far more deeply than the technical details of governmental economic policy, and that he saw the significance of the former in a much broader and less chauvinistic context.

In the course of the Exclusion controversy itself, and later in exile in Holland in the tolerant and sophisticated company of Dutch Arminian theologians and merchants and of some of the younger Huguenot refugees, he had come to see the interests of European Protestantism and those of political freedom as bound tightly together. The Catholic absolutism of Louis XIV, with its direct military menace to surviving Protestant States and its intractable commitment to religious uniformity, had come to symbolize politically all that Locke hated: the deep confusion between the arrogance, ambition, and corruption of human beings and the purposes of God. As soon as Locke entered Shaftesbury's household his views on the toleration of Dissenters from the Established Church shifted to a more relaxed and pragmatic attitude. In subsequent years the detachment fell away and he came to see (and, more importantly, to feel) the issue of toleration less and less as an issue of State policy and more and more as one of individual human right. In exile, for nearly six years, he had watched with growing fear the political and cultural, perhaps even the religious, future of Europe hang in the balance as the English Crown passed to a Catholic monarch and as Louis XIV threatened to overrun the last major bastion of Continental Protestantism in the Netherlands, revoked the Edict of Nantes, and settled down to crush the Huguenot Church and literally to dragoon its hapless adherents into the Catholic faith. (This last episode was sufficiently dramatic to add a verb to the English language.) It was in response to these events, to counter a peril which was European and not merely English, that he wrote the *Letter on Toleration*, which, unlike any of the other books that he published in his own lifetime, was first printed in the Latin which still served as the international language of European intellectuals.

EPISTOLA

de

TOLERANTIA

ad

Clariffimum Virum

T. A. R. P. T. O. L. A.

Scripta à

P. A. P. O. I. L. A.

per Joh. Lock

GOUDÆ,

Apud JUSTUM AB HOEVE,

cIɔ Iɔc Lxxxix,

5. Locke's first public defence of the right to religious toleration. Note the (anonymous) Dutch publication, the discreet dedication to his friend Limborch, and the equally discreet Latin affirmation of his own identity as a lover of peace, a hater of persecution, and an Englishman.

By 1689 the 'Protestant wind' had carried William of Orange safely across the Channel and the balance had at last begun to dip in the direction which Locke desired. The *Letter* was translated into English by a Unitarian merchant, William Popple; and, as we have already seen, it was published in England later in the same year that it had first appeared in Holland. Its insistence that any human attempt to interfere with religious belief or worship was blasphemously presumptuous was far more extreme than the modest concessions to the Dissenters which William and his government thought it prudent to make. In April of the next year the *Letter* was attacked at length in print by an Oxford cleric, Jonas Proast, the first of Locke's works to receive this honour. In the next few years Locke published two lengthy replies to Proast, and the latter, in each case, replied once more himself.

Locke remained, however, not merely unwilling to disclose his authorship of the *Letter* and the *Two Treatises*, but more than a little hysterical when friends incautiously or inadvertently threatened to disclose it for him. Even Limborch, to whom he was genuinely devoted, was savaged for acknowledging Locke's authorship of the *Letter* to other mutual friends in Holland, while the unfortunate Tyrrell, with whom Locke's relationship had grown increasingly testy, was brutally reprimanded for ascribing the *Two Treatises* to him. As late as 1698 (though admittedly under highly embarrassing circumstances) Locke refused obdurately to admit in writing even to one of his closest and most trusted friends, William Molyneux, that he had indeed written the *Two Treatises*. There can be no doubt at all that by this time his authorship of these works was a matter of common knowledge, and it is clear, not merely from the terms of his will but from some remarkably coy instances of self-praise (W IV 602, 640), that he continued to his death to endorse at least the essentials of their arguments. In the case of the *Two Treatises*, moreover, he carefully supervised the printing of a second edition in the year 1694 and worked painstakingly over a further edition, incorporating some important additions, which did not appear until after his death.

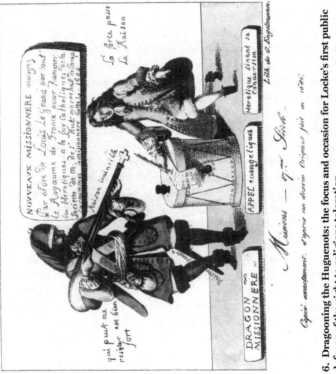

6. Dragooning the Huguenots: the focus and occasion for Locke's first public defence of the right to religious toleration.

In these years too he published a number of further works of some importance. Two of these, in 1691 and 1695, were concerned with the coinage. A third, *Some Thoughts concerning Education*, was issued in 1693 and went through three editions in the next few years. It had originated in a lengthy series of letters to a friend, the Somerset gentleman Edward Clarke, and to his wife Mary, advising them on the health and upbringing of their children. One of Locke's most accessible works, it shows a notably unsentimental view of a child's psychological development, both intellectually and morally. Besides the light it casts on Locke's conception of how a human being becomes fully human (principally by learning to control his or her less admirable desires), it seems also to have been of some historical importance in shaping English toilet-training practices, at least amongst the educated classes. In the case of these works Locke was decidedly less reluctant to acknowledge his authorship, though he did not in fact issue any of them initially under his own name. But in the case of his last unquestionably major work, *The Reasonableness of Christianity*, which appeared in 1695, he was once again determinedly secretive. As it turned out, he had good reason to be so, since the book proved extremely controversial, being attacked twice within two years by John Edwards for Socinianism, a recondite Continental heresy stressing the authority of reason and scripture which rejected the doctrine of the Trinity and which Edwards himself roundly equated with atheism. Locke replied to these attacks in two anonymous and somewhat disingenuous *Vindications* of his work. To make matters worse, in 1696 he was attacked once again on similar grounds by a far more formidable antagonist, none other than Edward Stillingfleet, the Anglican apologist for religious intolerance whom Locke and Tyrrell had worked together to refute during the Exclusion controversy, who now held the bishopric of Worcester.

The attack was especially damaging, not merely because the charge of Socinianism (unlike that of atheism) was an extremely plausible one to level at Locke's religious views, but also because Stillingfleet elected to press it not on the grounds of the *Reasonableness*, a text which Locke was by now most unlikely to acknowledge as his own, but rather on those of the *Essay*, a text which he could hardly in principle have repudiated since it was published under his own name, and which in any case he keenly desired to defend. He duly replied to Stillingfleet too, in three further works in 1697. Apart from the amendments to the fourth edition of the *Essay* which appeared in 1700, these replies in effect constituted his last public intellectual appearance in his lifetime.

By this stage of his life Locke's concerns were beginning to narrow and it becomes possible to pick out more clearly the strategy and tactics of his own custody of his intellectual legacy. We must postpone until the next two chapters a detailed assessment of the scope and limits of his intellectual achievement. But it may be illuminating to consider here in outline some of the more public tensions within that legacy and the practical implications which followed from them.

At his death Locke at last assumed full responsibility for all his published works. But until then, as we have seen, he remained anxious to segregate the *Essay*, a work of philosophy which he had always acknowledged as his own, from his anonymous writings on politics and religion. We do not know very clearly why he was so anxious to keep these apart. Perhaps, indeed, he did not know especially clearly himself. But one likely reason is the simple recognition, strongly confirmed from 1690 onwards, that the difficulty of retaining control over opinions expressed in one work is greatly accentuated by juxtaposing them with related opinions on further topics, expressed in one or more other works. Defending or improving the *Essay* was an ample assignment in itself; and Locke was always, with good reason, confident that it was the *Essay* that was his great achievement.

The theory of knowledge set out in the *Essay* is in some ways extremely sceptical. Locke himself did not regard it as in any way impugning the truth of Christian belief. But most of his contemporaries were hardly in a position to share his confidence since, if the arguments of the *Essay* were true, the particular interpretations of Christianity which they happened themselves to believe were certainly false. By the same token, Locke's sceptical view of man's capacity to know and his vigorous emphasis on the duty to tolerate religious beliefs which one happens to disbelieve and dislike might be natural partners in someone whose own religious convictions are clear and strong. But in anyone whose own religious convictions were less substantial, their union might seem alarmingly arbitrary and unstable. If Locke's reasons for insisting on religious tolerance were distinctively religious reasons (and reasons which led him to withhold toleration both from Catholics and from atheists), the consequences of his insistence, together with the later influence of his conception of man's capacity to know, might readily be (and largely were) to weaken religious conviction in others. This danger, of course, was one on which his critics were from the beginning eager to insist – and not merely in the form of Edwards's gutter polemics or Stillingfleet's ecclesiastical hauteur, but also of intellectual assessments of real weight such as that of the great German philosopher Leibniz. On the question of toleration in particular, Locke might well have seen by the date of his death the extreme political instability of his position between an authoritarian Anglicanism (such as Stillingfleet's), which was simply a pale shadow of the Sun King's absolutist pretensions, and the cheerily licentious deism of men like John Toland who claimed unabashedly to be pursuing the implications of Locke's theory of knowledge. As Locke advocated it, religious freedom was freedom to be religious in one's own way. It was emphatically not, as Toland gleefully took it to be, freedom to be utterly indifferent to religious considerations.

A comparable difficulty arose in the year 1698 over the conception of political duty set out in the *Two Treatises*. Locke's close friend William Molyneux was a Member of the Irish Parliament, which was at that time in conflict with the English House of Commons over the latter's entitlement to control the Irish economy and prevent its products from competing with those of England. Locke himself was closely concerned with the formulation of English State policy on the question through his membership of the Board of Trade. In 1698 Molyneux published a book on the issue, *The Case of Ireland*, which was to become one of the classic texts of Irish nationalism. In it he argued that for one country to legislate for another was incompatible with the theory of political rights set out in the *Two Treatises*. The work caused sufficient offence to be burnt by order of the House of Lords; and within months Molyneux came to England to meet for the first time, and to stay with, his friend. We do not, unfortunately, have any idea what they said to each other about the matter. But the meeting is dramatic enough even without such knowledge. For Molyneux's arguments about the implications of Locke's political theory paralleled very closely the arguments of the American colonists in the 1760s and 1770s; and whatever Locke did have to say in reply would apply directly enough to the use which American pamphleteers and spokesmen, from James Otis to Thomas Jefferson, were to make of his text. More interestingly still, as one of Molyneux's critics pointed out, in the case of Ireland, what Locke's theory implied (if it applied at all) was not that the resident English Protestant gentry in the Dublin Parliament had a right to control the economy of the country in which they lived, but rather that the native Catholic Irish had a right to do so. It is hard to think of a conclusion less likely to appeal to Locke, with his deep dislike of Catholicism and his nervous sense of the geopolitical vulnerability of European Protestantism. (The year 1698 was only eight years after the Battle of the Boyne, the most important military engagement which William III had had to face in consolidating his hold on the English Crown.) The political liberty that Locke had sought to vindicate in the *Two Treatises* was a liberty for Protestants within the British State. There is no reason to believe that he would have been reluctant to extend it to foreign Catholics in foreign Catholic States. What it emphatically was not intended to be was a liberty for Irish Catholics from the British Crown.

Some of the impact of Locke's writings was simply a product of the

Victoire Remportée par LE ROY GUILLAUME III. sur les Irlandois à la Riuiere de Boyne en Irlande 1. Iuillet 1690.

Depuis, après la Bataux, et pour forçer le Roy et Gasne par Thurler Maas.

7. The Battle of the Boyne, July 1690, William's initial military victory in Ireland, and still the emblem of Protestant triumph over the presumed threat of Catholicism.

arguments which they contained; and if the impact they made was not always an impact which he would have desired, all complicated thought is potentially subject to this hazard. But some – perhaps especially in the case of the *Essay* – was also a product of the form in which his writings reached readers and of the particular range of readers whom they reached. In England the *Essay* made its own way and made it with some rapidity, forcing itself upon the attention of even the universities (which were generally hostile to novel ideas, particularly those which they took to be theologically subversive) in the course of the author's lifetime. But the channels through which it reached a European public were rather narrower and more distinct. The first appearance of any part of the *Essay* in print was a French abridgement, issued in Amsterdam as a separate pamphlet in February 1688 but originally prepared for, and also included within, a leading intellectual journal, the *Bibliothèque Universelle*. Most of Locke's subsequent works were also reviewed at length in one or other of the variety of intellectual periodicals which were published in the Netherlands over the next few decades and edited in their earlier years for the most part by French Protestant refugees like Pierre Bayle and Jean Le Clerc. Since the diffusion of several of these journals was remarkably broad, Locke's works reached a wide intellectual public, particularly in France, comparatively quickly. A second important channel of diffusion, also a consequence of Locke's relations with French Protestantism, was more accidental and personal. Jean Barbeyrac, a French Protestant refugee, had exchanged letters with him in the last few years of his life. Early in the 18th century Barbeyrac began his great series of translations and critical editions of Grotius, Pufendorf, and other leading European texts on the Law of Nature. In these, for the first time, he offered a full and very carefully judged summary of the implications of Locke's philosophy and political writings for the central issues of ethics and politics. For several decades these texts were probably read more widely in many European countries than any other modern writings on ethics and politics; and they were at the centre of a major branch of law teaching in a wide array of British and European universities. Just as Locke's own most

Locke

important philosophical thinking was first prompted by Descartes and Gassendi, the scope of his European experiences and friendships guaranteed that its intellectual impact was in no danger of being confined to the British Isles.

In the last decade and a half of his life, as an old, sick, and immensely distinguished man, he was at last in a position to see more clearly the shape of his life as a whole and to sense the scale and meaning of his achievement. At the centre of this achievement lay the experience and the labours of his exile. At Shaftesbury's right hand Locke had been competing for public office and political power in his own country, living what even Machiavelli would have seen as a life of political virtue. When he returned from exile in 1689 he continued to discharge his political responsibilities. But in exile, for the first time in his life, he had acquired other and more pressing responsibilities. They had come essentially from his change of mind on the question of toleration. If freedom or restriction of religious practice was simply a matter of State policy, like foreign trade or defence, religious policy and civic virtue could not be seriously at odds. But if the right to worship God in one's own way was an individual right against any possible State power, the limits of religious policy were too important and too puzzling to be left to the crude judgement of civic virtue. With the massive intellectual labours of his exile, the *Letter* and the *Essay*, Locke had come to put his trust not in English nationalism and the political fortunes of the English State, but in working through, and making more accessible to other human beings, a culture of shared religious good intentions. He continued, certainly, to do his best, despite exhaustion and illness, to make the world in general and England in particular a safer setting for this culture. But his main energies were devoted to the construction and fuller understanding of the culture itself, to exploring how exactly human capabilities could enable men to live in tune with God's world and to know that they were doing so. In this effort he depended very heavily on the emotional support of his friends Limborch and William Molyneux, and on younger men such as the deist Anthony Collins and the future Lord

Chancellor Peter King. Shared religious good intentions were easier to trust than purely private hopes. But he also depended, and needed to depend, on at least one purely private hope, the hope that the better this culture was understood the easier it would be to believe in it and to live it. His hope remained very much a faith in a human future, not the future of a particular political unit but that of a potential civilization of indefinite geographical scope and historical duration.

Great historical movements are never the product of a single person's achievements. But there is a real justice in seeing the European Enlightenment as Locke's legacy: both his triumph and his tragedy. As it turned out, the culture which he wished to fashion did not become easier to believe in and to live the better it was understood. Instead it fragmented alarmingly. Shared religious good intentions gave way to shared secular good intentions; and the latter, too, gave way to violent and acrimonious wranglings over which secular intentions truly are good. The clearer his view of what men can know became, the less convincing became his view of how they have good reason to live their lives. If the Enlightenment was genuinely his legacy, it was scarcely the legacy which he wished to leave.

We are all of us the children of his failure.

Chapter 2
The politics of trust

In the year 1660 Locke composed his first two major writings (now commonly known as the *Two Tracts on Government*), a tract in English, *Question: Whether the Civill Magistrate may lawfully impose and determine the use of indifferent things in reference to Religious Worship*, and a briefer but more systematic Latin work on the same theme.

It was also in 1660 that Charles II was at last restored to the English throne, 11 years after his father's trial and death on the scaffold, when he returned to England from exile, determined never to go on his travels again. In the preceding 20 years a succession of English governments had sought to impose a wide variety of religious practices upon their recalcitrant subjects, always offending many and usually giving pleasure to remarkably few. Political disorder and religious dispute had been inextricably linked, leaving the great majority of the nation weary of the incessant wranglings and eager for peace and settlement. Locke's *Tracts* certainly echo the mood of this year, and they confront an issue which had been central to religious and political controversy in the turbulent decades which led up to it. The detail of their arguments is of little significance. But it is important to understand the main outline of the issue which they treated and to identify the difficulties which this issue presented to the young Locke.

The issue itself was eminently practical. In a society in which virtually everyone believed in the truth of the Christian religion but in which there were profound differences of opinion about how to practise it, who should decide which religious practices were to be permitted and which were to be prohibited? Should there, for example, be a single Christian Church, sponsored by the political authorities, to which every subject would be compelled to belong and within which he would be forced to worship in the forms which it prescribed? Or should religious worship, since it was properly the expression of sincere religious belief, be a matter purely for the conscience of each individual, a private transaction between him and his God, to be shaped as each believer felt appropriate? It is difficult for any Christian wholly to deny the force of either of these conceptions, and each receives some textual support from the New Testament. Locke himself at this time clearly felt the force of both, of authenticity as well as order and decency. But he had no difficulty in deciding the priority between the two.

If only religion in practice could safely be left to private choice, 'if men would suffer one another to go to heaven every one his own way, and not out of a fond conceit of themselves pretend to greater knowledge and care of one another's soul and eternal concernments than he himself', this might indeed 'promote a quiet in the world, and at last bring those glorious days that men have a great while sought after the wrong way' (G 161). But 20 years of religious wranglings had shown the peril of such tolerance. Almost 'all those tragical revolutions which have exercised Christendom these many years have turned upon this hinge, that there hath been no design so wicked which hath not worn the vizor of religion, nor rebellion which hath not been so kind to itself as to assume the specious name of reformation . . . none ever went about to ruin the *state* but with pretence to build the temple' (160). It was the confusion of 'ambition and revenge' with 'the cause of God' that had devastated England (161). To set the claims of authenticity above those of decency was to foment political disorder. And in 1660, like most of his fellow-countrymen, Locke was deeply afraid of political disorder.

It was not only on the national political stage, moreover, that the claims of decency and authenticity clashed. The immediate stimulus for Locke's English tract was a work by his fellow Student of Christ Church, Edmund Bagshaw, *The Great Question Concerning Things Indifferent in Religious Worship*, published in September of 1660. Bagshaw was a vehement exponent of the claims of authenticity at a time when the College's religious practices were being drastically restored to an Anglican orthodoxy of which he strongly disapproved. Surplices and the organ were reintroduced into Christ Church in November, while in January of the following year Bagshaw's supporters in the College stole as many of the surplices as they could get their hands on and deposited them in the College sewers. Both locally and nationally Locke espoused the claims of authority, stressing the gross untrustworthiness of the majority of mankind, at worst a real threat of anarchy and at best a formidable impediment to decency. The political views which he advanced were crude and evasive. What is interesting about them is their firm subordination of religious sentiment to the demands of politics. Whatever its origins, political authority, to be adequate to its tasks, must be total. God made the world and men in such a way that this is so; and, hence, it must be his will that political authority be unrestricted by anything but his express commands. 'Things indifferent' are all matters about which God has not naturally or by revelation made known his will. (The desirability or otherwise of wearing surplices, for example, was a matter about which few even amongst Anglicans supposed that God had made known his will.) No Christian political theorist could deny to an individual the right to believe his own beliefs. Religious ceremonies are in themselves not matters of belief but simply of practice. Good Christians should do what the magistrate tells them, and believe what they themselves believe. The problem, plainly, came when they happened to believe that they ought not at any price to do as the magistrate had commanded them. In the case of

Charles R.

Right Reverend Father in God, and Trusty
and Wellbeloved We greet you well. Whereas
We have received information of the factious
and disloyall behaviour of   Lock
one of the Students of that Our Colledge; We
have thought fit hereby to signify Our Will
and Pleasure to you, that you forthwith
remove him from his said Students Place,
and deprive him of all the Rights and
Advantages thereunto belonging. For
which this shall be your Warrant. And
so We bid you heartily farewell. Given
at Our Court at Whitehall the 11th day
of November 1684 in the Six & thirtieth
yeare of Our Reigne

By his Majtis command

Sunderland

Deane & Chapter of Christ church.

8. A letter concerning the expulsion of John Locke from Christ Church.

religious ceremonies it was a problem which came with some frequency. The conception of 'indifferent things' could not in principle settle it and Locke's tracts accordingly also failed to resolve it. It was also a problem which the Anglican Church at the Restoration singularly failed to solve in practice.

At this point Locke himself had dealt with the issue largely by ignoring it. Religious ceremonies simply were 'indifferent', a matter for human discretion. Anything that was simply a matter for human discretion could be decided authoritatively by the civil magistrate, because the purpose of having a magistrate at all was precisely to override the wilful partiality of each man's personal judgement. Peace required civil authority, and civil authority, in order to secure peace, could do anything whatever which God himself had not expressly prohibited. None of this, plainly, cast much light on what, specifically, the civil authority ought to do.

The *Essay on Toleration*

Seven years later, having escaped from the musty world of the Oxford don into the glamour and excitement of Shaftesbury's service, Locke considered these questions a second time from a very different angle and came to markedly different conclusions. These can be found in the *Essay on Toleration*, which, unlike the famous *Letter on Toleration*, was never published by Locke himself. The practical verdict which he reached in this *Essay* was very much that of Shaftesbury: toleration promotes civil order and harmony by 'making the terms of church communion as large as may be' (FB I 194). It is still the responsibility of the sovereign magistrate to regulate religious practice for the peace, safety, and security of his people. But although the magistrate remains firmly the judge of what will promote these ends, his judgement is no longer expected to be any more trustworthy in practice than that of any other believer. He

> ought still to have a great care that no such laws be made, no such restraints established, for any other reason but because the necessity

of the state and the welfare of the people called for them, and perhaps it will not be sufficient that he barely thinks such impositions and such rigour necessary or convenient unless he hath seriously and impartially considered and debated whether they be so or no; and his opinion (if he mistake) will no more justify him in the making of such laws than the conscience or opinion of the subject will excuse him if he disobey them, if consideration and inquiry could have better informed either of them. (FB I 180)

The range over which the magistrate has discretion remains as broad as the whole field of 'indifferent things'; but his exercise of this discretion is governed rigorously by the end which he exists to serve. If he acts, as best he can, to carry out the duties which follow from this end, he will not even 'be accountable in the other world for what he does directly in order to the preservation and peace of his people, according to the best of his knowledge' (I 185). But if he attempts to meddle with the religious convictions as such of his subjects (as the Anglican authorities were certainly attempting to interfere with those of the Dissenters), his actions will be as unjust as they are absurd. Each individual is responsible for his own salvation; and no one could have good reason to entrust his salvation to the necessarily incompetent discretion of another human being (I 176–7). In any case and more decisively, even if he wished to do so, it is quite simply the case that no one *can* do so. No

man can give another man power . . . over that over which he has no power himself. Now that a man cannot command his own understanding or positively determine today what opinion he will be of tomorrow, is evident from experience and the nature of the understanding, which cannot more apprehend things otherwise than they appear to it, than the eye see other colours in the rainbow than it doth, whether these colours be really there or no. (I 176)

The *Essay on Toleration* is an argument addressed to a sovereign on how he should employ his discretion. It carefully avoids the least hint that subjects have any right to a discretion of their own in the face of the sovereign's commands. The duty of subjects is to obey passively. But already, within the field of indifferent things, Locke has marked out a zone in which passive obedience is simply impossible. Still more decisively, he has made it clear that this zone crosses the borders of the field of indifferent things. Human belief cannot submit to the claims of authority; and it cannot be true for any human being that he has good reason to abandon his own beliefs about what God requires of him at the command of another human being. It is as holders of beliefs, and most decisively as holders of religious beliefs, that human beings are equal with one another: both 'the multitude that are as impatient of restraint as the sea . . . whom knowing men have always found and therefore called beasts' (G 158), and the rulers whom they so urgently need to restrain their fraud and violence towards one another (FB I 174). Each is fully responsible for his own beliefs and will have to answer for them to God at the Last Judgement. But, in the mean time, it is the business of the magistrate to attend rigorously to the necessity of preserving civil order, not to try to stand in, unavailingly and impertinently, for the Deity. It is no longer difficult to see how, in the very different circumstances of the Exclusion controversy and faced by a hostile and vindictive ruler, the duty of passive obedience would come to seem to Locke a vicious absurdity.

The *Two Treatises of Government*

We do not know when exactly Locke wrote the *Two Treatises of Government*. We do not even know for certain how much of it he wrote for the first time (or rewrote extensively) shortly before he published it in 1689. Indeed we do not really possess decisive proof that he wrote any of it in the course of the Exclusion controversy. But the most imaginative and scholarly writers to consider the question in recent decades have agreed on at least two points. First, Locke had written the great bulk of the text which he published in 1689 by the time that he left the country for Holland late in the summer of 1683. Secondly, he had written different passages in the book (as this stood in 1683) over a number of years previously, and the text accordingly reflects a number of the changing positions which Shaftesbury's party had adopted in the course of this dispute.

As we have it today, the *Two Treatises* is a work principally designed to assert a right of resistance to unjust authority, a right, in the last resort, of revolution. (There are, of course, on any reading many other major themes of the book: an account of what makes governments legitimate in the first place (the theory of consent) and of how subjects and rulers ought to interpret their relations with each other (the theory of trust); an account of how human beings can become entitled to own economic goods and of the extent and limits of their title to do so (the theory of property); an account of the similarities and differences between different types of human authority, and above all of the differences between authority in a family and authority in a State. All of these questions, too, are considered in the context of English politics at the time and of English constitutional doctrine.) It is clear enough that, even from the first, the *Two Treatises* attacked the pretensions of absolute monarchy and that it drew firm conclusions from this attack about the constitutional limits on the prerogative powers of the King of England. But it is certainly not clear that when Locke began to write it his intention was to defend a right of active disobedience on the part of the elected House of Commons, let alone the possession and use of such a right by individual aggrieved subjects with no formal position of authority in their society.

The *Two Treatises* is a long and complex work which contains a great many arguments. Most of these, naturally, were arguments which Locke had not previously advanced elsewhere. But only in the case of the right of resistance did he explicitly and decisively reverse a theoretical view which he had defended at length in earlier works. Both in the *Tracts* of 1660 and in the *Essay on Toleration* of 1667 the duty of a subject in the face of the unjust commands of his sovereign was clearly asserted to be to obey these commands passively: not of course in any sense to endorse their justice, but at

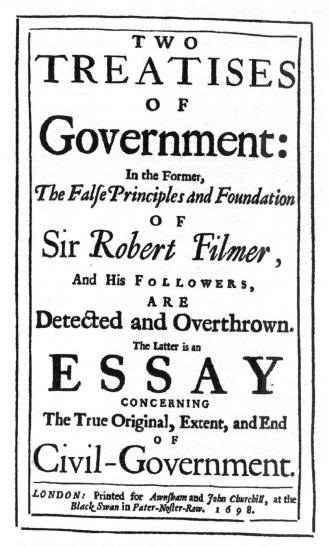

TWO
TREATISES
OF
Government:

In the Former,
The False Principles and Foundation

OF

Sir *Robert Filmer*,

And His FOLLOWERS,
ARE
Detected and Overthrown.

The Latter is an

ESSAY

CONCERNING

The True Original, Extent, and End

OF

Civil-Government.

LONDON: Printed for *Awnsham* and *John Churchill*, at the Black Swan in *Pater-Noster-Row.* 1 6 9 8.

9. Asserting the Right of Resistance: Locke's *Two Treatises of Government*. Note the absence of an author's name, even eight years after its initial publication.

least to recognize the authority from which they issued and certainly not at any price to obstruct them forcibly, let alone to attack their author. As recently as 1676 he had argued once more that, although human political authorities are designated by human laws, the duty of political obedience is laid down by the law of God 'which forbids disturbance or dissolution of governments', and that every human being is obliged in good conscience to obey the government under which he or she lives (D 49 n.).

The impetus behind this change of mind plainly followed directly from Locke's own political involvement in the years of the book's composition. It was a fundamental shift in intellectual judgement as well as in political commitment; and Locke set himself to think through its implications with great thoroughness. He did not, of course, consider systematically the implications of all the views which he asserted in his book. In particular he chose not to discuss at all the question of how men can naturally know the law of nature, the binding law of God, on which, according to the argument of the book, all human rights rested and from which the great bulk of human duties more or less directly derived. The omission has attracted much intellectual criticism from later writers on political theory. It has also earned, both at the time of publication and more recently, some suspicion that the pious tone of its discussion of the law of nature might have been evasive or insincere. What is certain is that already in his 1664 lectures on the law of nature at Christ Church he had identified some of the main difficulties in the traditional Christian conception of natural law, and that he had, if anything, sharpened his understanding of these difficulties in the course of his preliminary work, recorded in the drafts of 1671, for the *Essay concerning Human Understanding*. By 1680, for example, he was certainly aware that the question of how men can *know* the content of the law of nature was deeply problematic. Yet in the *Two Treatises* he writes as though, however complete their freedom to choose whether or not to obey, *knowledge* of the law of nature was virtually compulsive for all men: 'so plain was it writ in the hearts of all mankind'.

On the whole these suspicions are beside the point. There is no doubt at all that Locke's attempt to explain how men can know the law of nature was in the end a failure even in his own eyes. But there is strong evidence that he persisted in this attempt for several years after the publication of the first edition of the *Essay* in 1689, and it is absurd to doubt that he did so because he continued to hope that the attempt might succeed. It is clear, too, that he did not, at this or any other period of his life, find at all attractive the uncompromisingly secular conception of natural law as a theory of purely human convenience adopted, for example, by Thomas Hobbes. A more attractive possibility, which he explored later in *The Reasonableness of Christianity*, would have been to rest human duties and rights directly on the revealed doctrines of Christianity. But even if he had supposed it possible, with the great French theologian Bossuet, to draw the principles of politics directly from the very words of the holy scriptures, it could scarcely have served Shaftesbury's political purposes in the struggle against Charles II to attempt anything of the kind. From the point of view of a modern unbeliever there is every reason to doubt the cogency of the political theory which Locke advances in the *Two Treatises*, because of its abject dependence on a view of man's place in nature as one in which each man is fully instructed by the Deity on how he ought to live. For most people today (including a great many devout Christians) such a view is barely intelligible. But there is no historical reason whatever to doubt that it was Locke's view.

For him, political rights follow from political duties and both derive from God's will. As he asked rhetorically in 1678: 'If he finds that God has made him and other men in a state wherein they cannot subsist without society, can he but conclude that he is obliged and that God requires him to follow those rules which conduce to the preserving of society?' (D 49 n.). The pivotal change in his political views, from a commitment to passive obedience to a vindication of the right of resistance to unjust political authority, was a change in his conception of how men could and should judge what is capable of preserving their society. Instead of leaving this judgement entirely to the ruler and retaining for the rest of the population merely the right to believe their own religious beliefs (a right which in any case he supposed that they had no power to abandon), Locke in the *Two Treatises* returned the right and duty of judging how to preserve society to every adult human being. It was in no sense an unprecedented conclusion. But for Locke himself it was certainly a very drastic change of mind.

How exactly should we see his reasons for this change? The most immediate pressure, clearly, was the directly political experience of the Exclusion controversy. There is no reason to believe that Locke would have written a work of political theory that at all resembled the *Two Treatises*, had it not been for Shaftesbury's role in this political struggle. Both the occasion of and the motive for its composition make the *Two Treatises* an Exclusion tract. But in a number of ways it was poorly designed as such – and not merely because of its original length, more than twice that of the published text, as the Preface to the Reader tells us. Even on constitutional questions which were of immediate importance at the time, Locke's arguments and Shaftesbury's tactics sometimes diverged widely. But quite apart from such details of practical political judgement, the character of the book as a whole makes it clear that Locke was thinking through the implications of his own change of mind, not simply writing up an extended brief for his factious master. It was Locke's own political experience at the time which altered the way in which he saw politics. Above all, it altered how he saw the relation between politics and the rest of human life. And it was the vigour with which he attempted to understand the implications of his own change of mind which made the *Two Treatises* a great work of political theory.

No doubt, more or less chance political experiences of just such a kind stand behind most of the great works of political theory. It is natural enough for the stimulus to think even very deeply about politics to be crudely political. But in the case of the *Two Treatises* the chance circumstances of its composition intrude further and more puzzlingly into the text of the work itself. The *First Treatise* is a lengthy criticism of the political writings of an earlier political writer, the Kentish squire Sir Robert Filmer, a royalist writer of the Civil-War period. Filmer was a thinker of some critical ability. As we have already seen, two other Exclusion tracts, by James Tyrrell and Algernon Sidney, had taken the form of attacks on Filmer's works. There was, therefore, nothing eccentric about Locke's choice of a target. Filmer stood out from other royalist ideologues, dead and living, by the uncompromising character of his theory of political authority, devout enough in tone and premises to reassure any Anglican, but also sufficiently absolute in its claims to match the practical appeals of the distressingly less devout theory of Thomas Hobbes. It is not altogether clear whether the choice of Filmer as an enemy in the early 1680s was a tribute to his popularity amongst supporters of Charles II or whether it was more a reflection of his attractions as an intellectual target. But here too what mattered for the quality and content of the book which Locke wrote was not the original motive which led him to undertake it, but the intellectual effect of organizing his thinking to such a large degree, in the *Second Treatise* as well as in the *First*, around an attack on Filmer.

The most important direct consequence of this focus was on his treatment of property, an achievement of which he was clearly extremely proud (W IV 640). But perhaps even more important was the imaginative impact upon his book as a whole of confronting such a vivid rendering of the view of politics which Locke himself had come to reject so very recently. In the political context of the Exclusion controversy and the social context of late 17th-century England before and afterwards, it is clear that Locke's political views were not unusually radical. He neither expected, nor, as far as we know, would he even have desired, a realization in his day of the radical programmes for extending the right to vote put forward by the Levellers in the English Civil War or by the Chartist movement a century and a half after him. But the theory which he set out in the

Two Treatises was a very radical theory, a theory of political equality and responsibility, resting on the judgement of each individual adult; and, at intervals throughout the book, Locke himself expressed the theory as though he meant it to be taken literally. For the audience which he supposed himself to be addressing, there was little danger of his being so taken. (Most English adults at the time could scarcely have read and understood the *Two Treatises*.) Indeed it was for some time subsequently only his conservative critics who pretended to believe that he meant or deserved to be taken literally. But in due course the theory and even some of the slogans set out in the book were to reach a much wider audience in England and in America. When they did so, its radicalism became extremely hard to deny. The clarity and force with which that radicalism was set out in the *Two Treatises* was largely a product of Locke's own imaginative response to the challenge of Filmer.

That challenge was at its most intellectually effective in its criticism of political theories which sought to derive political authority and rights of ownership from the free choices of human beings. Despite its ideological resonance, it was distinctly less impressive as a theory of legitimate authority in its own right. The essence of Filmer's view was bizarrely simple; and even to some of his contemporaries it plainly appeared more than a little quaint. All authority amongst human beings, he believed, was essentially of the same kind, the authority of a father in his family and the authority of a monarch in his kingdom. All authority of one human being over another was given directly by God. Since no human being had a right over his own life and since all human rulers had a right to take the lives of their own subjects or of foreign enemies when these in their judgement had sufficiently damaged the public good, it must follow that rulers derived this right not from their subjects but from God himself. The Christian prohibition on suicide and the rights of a sovereign could be compatible with each other only on the assumption that the rights of the sovereign were given to him by the Deity. The Christian scriptures (or, to be more accurate, the Old Testament) record the precise occasion of this gift. God gave the whole earth to the first man, Adam, and all political authority and all rights of ownership are a historical and legal consequence of that gift. Adam's dominion was a fact of history which only the impious (or those unfortunate enough never to have encountered the Christian revelation) could have any occasion to deny. From the time of this first disposition of the world, Adam's dominion, a form of ownership of things as well as a form of rule over men, had become much subdivided by the course of human history. But every subdivision had been a direct expression of God's providence and must be recognized as representing his will. The political responsibilities of any man (and still more so, those of any woman) who did not happen to be a ruler were simply to do what he was told, to recognize the providence of God in the political authority to which he found himself subject, and to honour and obey this authority accordingly. Filmer's statement of this view was neither clear nor economical. It seems most unlikely that many who did not already feel obliged to obey their ruler were convinced by reading it that they were obliged in conscience to do so.

But if his own theory lacked cogency, Filmer did raise a number of embarrassing problems for anyone who believed that the practical sources of political authority were purely human. Perhaps equally importantly, the form which his theory took presented the claims of absolute political authority in a memorably disagreeable light. Locke, as we have seen, had no difficulty in regarding political obedience as a very simple and fundamental duty for most men (and almost all women) at most times, a consequence of that law of God 'which forbids disturbance or dissolution of governments'. In the circumstances of the Exclusion controversy, of course, he had strong motives for reconsidering the scope and comprehensiveness of the duty and for questioning his earlier presumptions about what made it truly a duty. Filmer's writings simplified the issue for him obligingly, offering a precise doctrine which he found it extremely easy to reject. For Filmer the rights of rulers are a personal gift from God. They are to be understood essentially as rights of ownership, over human beings as well as over land and material goods. Subjects belong to their ruler and owe obedience to him because God has, through the workings of his providence, given them to him. In reply Locke sought to distinguish sharply between the duties of subjects to obey and the rights of rulers to command. Most of the time in societies most men would have a duty to obey because civil peace and order are preconditions for the living of a decent human life. But rulers, by contrast, would have a right to command only where their exercise of power and the commands which they issued deserved obedience. If rulers themselves threatened civil peace and order, their subjects would have every right to judge the degree and immediacy of the threat and, if this seemed sufficiently serious, to resist it as best they could. Filmer, then, gave Locke just what he wished to deny: a clear practical equation of the all too human incumbents of political authority with the will of God himself. But he also set Locke several difficult intellectual problems. Two of these stood out with particular starkness: that of reconciling a purely human origin for political authority with the right to take human life and with the record of secular and sacred history; and that of explaining how human beings could come to have an individual property in any part of God's earth or its produce.

The problem of the right to property

The question of property was especially challenging. Filmer's own criticisms had been directed against the most influential 17th-century theory of property right, that advanced by the great Dutch natural-law writer Hugo Grotius. Filmer saw Grotius as proclaiming two inconsistent ideas, the view that non-human nature belonged to all human beings in common and the view that individual men or women could come by agreement privately to own parts of it. What made the two ideas plainly inconsistent, in his eyes, was the discontinuity which they implied in God's laws for men in the two contrasting situations, in one of which he had apparently 'ordained community' and in the other of which he had prescribed private ownership. For anyone with a more sophisticated sense of the historical development of human society this objection was unimpressive. But on the basis of it Filmer advanced two further lines of criticism which were less easy to shrug off. First, he probed at some length the historical plausibility of the sequence envisaged by Grotius in which the human species as a whole (or some portion of it in a particular locality) must have come together and agreed unanimously to divide up ownership over all that they collectively possessed. If property is a matter of right and if all men originally owned everything together, then no man could lose his right to everything (or anything) without consciously choosing to abandon it. Secondly, he questioned whether even the unanimous consent of all living human beings at a particular time could bind any subsequent human beings who had not themselves been a party to the agreement, or whether, indeed, even such unanimous consent would necessarily bind any of the original contractors who subsequently changed his mind about its merits. For Filmer, property could only be practically secure and legally valid, if, like political authority itself, it were the direct expression of the will of God. Once it was seen as resting on human decision and commitment, any right was open to indefinite revision. On this point at least, Locke was largely in agreement with him. It was the question of how existing rights to property could be guaranteed under a government chosen by the people as a whole on which the Leveller campaign in the Civil War had foundered. As Henry Ireton brutally demanded of the Leveller leaders at Putney in October 1647: 'I would very fain know what you gentlemen, or any other, do account the right you have to anything in England.' If political authority did not derive directly from God but instead rested on human choice, the idea of a right to property might seem alarmingly flimsy.

Locke's response to this threat is extremely subtle. He takes it as a truth both of human reason and of revelation that the earth, like its human inhabitants (T II 6), belongs to its Creator and that God has given it to these human inhabitants in common (II 25) and given it to them to enjoy (II 31). He dismisses the idea that there could be any right of private property at all on Filmer's presumption that

God had given the whole earth to 'Adam and his Heirs in Succession, exclusive of the rest of his Posterity' (II 25). But he sets himself to answer fully the main critical thrust of Filmer's attack on Grotius, the question of how men can come to have a private *right* to any part of this common heritage. It is his answer to this question which is famous and which has given his theory of property its immense and bewilderingly varied historical influence. Labour is what distinguishes what is privately owned from what is held in common; the labour of a man's body and the work of his hands. Labour is the unquestionable property of the labourer; and by mixing his labour with material objects – hunting (II 30), gathering (II 28), but also cultivating the ground (II 32–4) – a man acquires the right to what he has worked on and to what he has made of this material. The 'Condition of Humane Life, which requires Labour and Materials to work on, necessarily introduces private *Possessions*' (II 35). God gave the world to men 'for their benefit, and the greatest Conveniencies of Life they were capable to draw from it'. But he gave it to them to use well by their exertions – 'to the use of the Industrious and Rational' and 'not to the Fancy or Covetousness of the Quarrelsome and Contentious' (II 34). The industrious and rational are *obliged* to make good use of it. It is not simply theirs, to do with precisely as they fancy. They are its stewards and must display their stewardship in their industry as well as in their rationality. They may appropriate and consume nature. (That is literally what nature is for.) But they have no right whatever to waste any of it. 'Nothing was made by God for Man to spoil or destroy' (II 31). In exercising their stewardship the industrious change the world which God originally gave to mankind, in a number of drastic ways. Labour is a creative activity. It '*puts the difference of value* on every thing' (II 40) and '*makes far the greatest part of the value* of things, we enjoy in this World' (II 42–3). Where labour has not been exerted effectively, as in an area like America, rich in land and furnished as liberally by nature 'with the materials of Plenty', the country will not have a hundredth part of the 'Conveniencies' enjoyed in 17th-century England. 'And a King of a large and fruitful Territory there feeds, lodges, and is clad worse than a day labourer in *England*' (II 41). Labour is a natural power of man and its exercise is commanded by God and encouraged by a rational understanding of man's place in nature. Its effects are almost wholly beneficial. It is as old as the Fall of Man. In 'the beginning all the World was America' (II 49); but by the 17th century much of it had been vastly improved by human labour. If labour is indeed the origin of property, then – at least at its origin, if not necessarily after the operation of inheritance – entitlement and merit are fused together; and the consequences for mankind as a whole can leave little ground for anxiety. At least initially, those who possess more will be those who deserve to do so and they will have nothing to apologize for to those who deserve and possess less.

But most of the world is America no longer – not simply because human labour has vastly increased its productivity, but also because human beings have discovered how to make possible a very different scale of economic inequality from that which the order of nature itself makes directly possible. Labour first begins '*a title of Property* in the common things of Nature' (II 51), a title bounded by use. In doing so it resolves the problem which Filmer set to Grotius. At this initial stage of human history property right was a simple and uncontentious matter. There 'could then be no reason of quarrelling about Title, nor any doubt about the largeness of Possession it gave. Right and conveniency went together; for as a Man had a Right to all he could imploy his Labour upon, so he had no temptation to labour for more than he could make use of' (II 51). The device which has made it possible for men to escape from this condition is the invention of money, a permanent store of value which 'being little useful to the Life of Man in proportion to Food, Rayment, and Carriage, has its value only from the consent of Men' (II 50). The invention of money greatly amplifies the inequality of possessions made possible by the 'different degrees of Industry' which men display (II 48). It makes it possible, in Locke's judgement, for a man *fairly* to 'possess more than he can use the product of', since he can hoard up, without injury to anyone, the value of the surplus which his property produces, in the form of gold and silver. Monetary exchange does not depend upon political authority; and economic inequality, which is a consequence of monetary exchange, does not depend for its legitimacy upon the civil law of a particular society (II 50).

Here Locke is pressing a very delicate case. In any political society, as he fully admits, property rights are regulated by the law (II 50). But it was essential for his purposes that such regulation could not justly be arbitrary, that it should instead be guided by the purposes for which governments properly exist and by the ends which give human beings rights over the material world at all. Property rights founded directly upon labour, in his eyes, neither required regulation by governments nor permitted much just modification by governments. But labour had done mankind nothing but good. The role of money was altogether more ambiguous. Money had introduced in full measure reasons for quarrelling about title, and doubts about largeness of possession. It was money which meant that right and conveniency no longer went together. The entire social and economic order of 17th-century England rested upon a human institution about whose moral status Locke felt deeply ambivalent. At this point in his theory, and without anachronism, we can see the moral fragility of commercial capitalism come briefly but sharply into focus. But we can see it so clearly, not because of our own superior insight or the advantages of hindsight, but because Locke himself felt so little inclination to deny it. What Locke's theory of property was for was not to put a good face on the social and economic order of the England of his day.

But what sort of right of property did he in fact wish to defend? It is easier to be certain – and may perhaps have been clearer to Locke himself – what sort of property he wished to deny. 'Property' in his vocabulary was the main term for expressing human entitlements. If there were no human entitlements there could be no injustice. To do injustice to a person is to take away from him something to which he has a right: for example, his life, his liberty or his material possessions. To protect human entitlements is the purpose of government. Government, then, exists to secure to all human beings their lives, their liberties and their material possessions. Every human being is certainly entitled to his own life and his own liberty, unless he forfeits these by violent assaults upon the lives and liberties of others. Entitlement to material possessions, however, was a more delicate matter. Material possessions which were a direct product of a man's labour were truly his; and there is no evidence that Locke felt the least qualm at the prospect of their being given to others in their owner's lifetime or passing to his heirs after his death (I 42). But where the scale of economic inequality depended solely upon a human convention, doubts about largeness of possession were harder to avoid. We do not really know with any precision what Locke did think about this question. But there are several points about which we can be confident.

The first is that the main stimulus which led him in chapter V of the *Second Treatise* to discuss property in our sense, entitlement to material possessions, was the wish to deny a right on the part of a reigning monarch to do as he chose with the material possessions of his subjects, without their express consent. The claim to exercise such a right, for the public good, by King Charles I had been one of the main precipitants of the English Civil War; and the possibility of its revival by his son was an important political threat to the Whigs in the Exclusion controversy. It was, furthermore, a right which Filmer had trenchantly defended. The initial appeal for Locke of founding entitlement to property upon labour was the directness with which it met this challenge. It was God, not human convention, that had given men a title to the fruits of their labour. Indeed it was only human convention that gave a monarch such authority as he held over his subjects. Instead of possessing a royal dominion over subjects and territory inherited directly from God's gift of the world to Adam, Locke's ruler had in the first instance simply the duty to use such power as was available to him to protect the rights which God himself had given directly to his subjects.

Locke was, of course, well aware, as his phrasing makes plain, that an immediate and transparent moral authority of possessions founded on physical effort did not (and could not be expected to) extend to the range of economic inequality produced by the operation of monetary exchange through a lengthy period of time. But what he needed, to refute royal claims to dispose of their subjects' possessions as they thought best, was not a theory of why every subject was fully and unequivocally entitled to everything which he legally owned, but simply an explanation of why private property could be (and often was) a right against even a legitimate political authority. Even on Locke's own account, to take away the fruits of a man's labour is a very different degree of injustice from taking away the profits of speculation, or taxing an aristocratic rent-roll which had reached its present owner by past brigandage or royal favouritism to a distant ancestor. But from Locke's own political point of view, of course, the latter possibilities were distinctly more urgent threats at the time; and there is no reason to believe that he would have *felt* any less disapproval in their case than in the former.

What is harder to assess is how exactly the theory of property which he had constructed appeared to him in retrospect, and particularly in the last few years of his life. We know, as already mentioned, that he felt some pride in it. But we do not know just which aspects of the theory gave him such satisfaction. The boldest answer to this question, advanced most strikingly by C. B. Macpherson, is that Locke intended his theory as an explanation of the moral legitimacy of capitalist production. There is little case for taking this seriously as an assessment of Locke's intentions in building his theory. But it is a more interesting question how far this suggestion may capture, if in mildly anachronistic terms, Locke's sense of his own achievement in having constructed his theory. In its strongest form the suggestion remains wholly unconvincing. Locke, like Thomas Aquinas, believed that all men had a right to physical subsistence which overrode the property rights of other humans. He believed that, even if the just price is the market price (V), to insist on selling only at the market price to a man in mortal need and to cause his death by doing so was to be guilty of murder. He believed that those who had worked hard all their lives had a right in their old age not merely to subsistence but to a decent standard of living. All of these were rights which rested directly upon God's gift of the world to men in common; and the idea that subsequent human conventions (like monetary exchange) might be entitled to entrench on them is fundamentally at odds with Locke's conception of property. He does, it is true, recognize that the paid labour of a servant can be owned by his master. But this comparatively casual acknowledgement of what was, after all, a fairly central feature of English economic relations in his day can hardly establish an enthusiasm for the central role of wage labour in capitalist production. In particular Locke denies explicitly that a man who has been deprived of the means of production (given by God to all men) can be forced into subjection through control over these means (T I 41–2).

> *Charity* gives every Man a Title to so much out of another's Plenty, as will keep him from Extream want, where he has no means to subsist otherwise; and a Man can no more justly make use of another's necessity, to force him to become his Vassal, by withholding that Relief, God requires him to afford to the wants of his Brother, than he that has more strength can seize upon a weaker, master him to his Obedience, and with a Dagger at his Throat offer him Death or Slavery. (I 42)

On the whole there is good reason to believe that Locke felt his account of property to be a major advance on the leading theorists of property rights, Grotius and Pufendorf, in explaining the system of rights on which a commercial society rested. But there is no reason to believe that he viewed this system of rights with undiscriminating enthusiasm. The productivity of human labour had transformed the world for man's enjoyment, as God had intended it to do. Monetary exchange, a purely human device, had in many ways assisted this transformation; but it had also clouded the moral transparency of human ownership beyond recall. Where entitlements that flow directly from labour clash with entitlements that rest solely on complex monetary exchanges, Locke himself would be ill placed to endorse the latter. The tangled history of the labour theory of value ever since, in the justification and rejection of capitalist production, was already foreshadowed in the ambiguities of the theory which he fashioned.

10. John Locke, 1676, by John Greenhill.

The nature of political authority

The second major challenge which Filmer's writings posed for Locke was in some ways easier to meet, and it certainly elicited from him a less original response. But since the question directly at issue in this case was the right of resistance to unjust political authority, Locke addressed it at much greater length and with far more rhetorical energy than he devoted to the topic of property rights. Filmer, as we have seen, believed that all subjects owed obedience to their ruler because God had quite literally given them, along with the territories in which they lived, to this ruler. The relation in which their ruler stood towards them was that of an owner. Locke himself in earlier years had taken a very favourable view of the claims of political authority. But there is no reason to believe that he would ever have found the uncompromising Filmerian doctrine at all attractive. He accepted the force of Filmer's emphasis on the centrality of the Christian prohibition on suicide in political theory. But he used it to attack Filmer's ideas at their core. Since men belong in the last instance not to themselves but to the God who made them, any human right to take away the life of any man (oneself included) must rest directly on God's purposes for men in general. The idea of one man owning another, let alone millions of others, by inheritance has no plausible link whatever with God's purposes for men. Filmer's arguments made all political subjects into slaves. Slavery was a condition into which extreme wickedness could justly cause a man to fall. But it was the opposite of a truly human life and it could not under any circumstances justly follow from the wicked actions of another person. (This proviso should have been extremely embarrassing for Locke himself in his capacity as stockholder of the slave-trading Royal Africa Company, since it clearly implied that the status of a slave could not legitimately be inherited from one generation to another. All legitimate servitude was intrinsically penal and the crimes of the father or mother could not descend to their children.) For Locke slavery was the precise opposite of legitimate political authority. What made political authority legitimate, what gave legitimate rulers the right to command, were the practical services which they could and did provide for their subjects. So far from being the owner of those whom they ruled, a legitimate monarch was essentially their servant.

For Filmer (as indeed for the young Locke) men were too stubborn, selfish, and quarrelsome to be left unaided to work out their own practical salvation. God's providence watched over them and it did so above all by subjecting them permanently to a grid of effective authority. Throughout his intellectual life Locke accepted this assessment of what men are like and of how they can be expected to behave. But with the *Two Treatises* he extended it confidently to rulers as much as to subjects, and drew from it implications very different from those which had occurred to Filmer. In his first writings there was a wide gulf between the godlike ruler and the multitude 'whom knowing men have always found and therefore called beasts' (G 158). But in the *Two Treatises* this gulf has disappeared and the ruler is seen as being just as likely as his subjects to enter upon 'force, the way of Beasts' (T II 181).

The opposite of force is reason. It is reason that distinguishes man from beast, and the way of reason is the way that God wills men to follow. It is through the exercise of their reason that men can and should know what God wills them to do; and it is their reason that enables them to judge what it would be best to do where God's will does not enter directly into the matter. All human adults who are not simply deranged have reason. All men are born free and rational, though these are potentialities which they must, through time, learn to exercise, not powers which they fully possess at their birth. As rational creatures of God, living within a world created by God, all men are equal with one another, equal in their fundamental entitlements, and equal too in the duties which they owe.

In this equality of right and duty, and independently of the actual histories of all times and places, human beings confront each other in what Locke calls the state of nature. This is probably the most misunderstood of all his ideas. Principally it has been misunderstood because of the role of a partially similar idea in the writings of Thomas Hobbes. Hobbes describes the natural condition of mankind as a state of violent conflict produced by passion and animosity from which man's reason alone has the power to rescue him. Fear of mortal danger is the only motive strong enough to overcome man's deeply antisocial qualities. Locke takes a less excitable view of the practical peril which men present to each other and recognizes social as well as antisocial features in human nature. But on the whole he does not differ widely from Hobbes (or indeed from Filmer) in his judgement of what men are like and how they can be expected to behave. But whereas in Hobbes the state of nature can in part be understood as a picture of how men would behave if they were not subjected to political authority, in Locke the phrase simply does not refer to human dispositions and attitudes at all. What the state of nature is for him is the condition in which God himself places all men in the world, prior to the lives which they live and the societies which are fashioned by the living of these lives. What it is designed to show is not what men are like but rather what rights and duties they have as the creatures of God.

Their most fundamental right and duty is to judge how the God who has created them requires them to live in the world which he has also created. His requirement for all men in the state of nature is that they live according to the law of nature. Through the exercise of his reason every man has the ability to grasp the content of this law. But although Locke was deeply convinced that human beings have the duty to understand this law and both the duty and the capacity to observe its requirements, he was by the early 1680s far from confident of how exactly they held and ought to exercise the capacity to understand it. As we shall see, the question of how men could distinguish the dictates of the law of nature from the prejudices prevailing in their own society preoccupied him throughout his intellectual life. In the *Two Treatises*, however, the question of how men could know the content of the law of nature was one which he could safely ignore. What mattered, simply, was their duty and capacity to observe it and their capacity, as free agents, to choose to break it. None of those against whom Locke was intending to argue at the time would have dissented from this judgement; and to have attempted to establish it in the course of his argument would have been as uneconomical and as intellectually taxing as, for example, attempting to prove the existence of a divine Creator in the same work.

In the state of nature the duties of each man under the law of nature are matched by the rights which he possesses under this law. The most important of these rights is the right to hold other men responsible for their breaches of this law and to punish them accordingly: the executive power of the law of nature which alone makes this law operative amongst human beings on earth. No man has a right to kill himself, because all men belong to God (a clear limit to the sense in which men have a property in their own bodies). But any man has a right to inflict penalties, up to and including the death penalty, on any other man who has violated nature's law drastically enough, and in particular on any other man who has without justification threatened the life of any human being. To spoil and waste any of God's gifts was an offence against nature's law. But to spoil or waste any human being was a crime of especial horror. The state of nature was a condition of equality and one in which, even in the civilized world of Locke's day, it was still on occasion possible for human beings to encounter one another. Wherever men met outside the framework of a common legitimate political authority, they too met, in this sense, as equals: a Swiss and an Indian in the woods of America, or a King of England and a King of France settling the fates of their countries on a field of cloth of gold. For Filmer, as indeed for many 18th-century critics of theories of natural rights, the state of nature was a fraudulent allegation about the human past, an apocryphal amendment to the scriptural record or a piece of wholly fictitious profane history. But for Locke, of course, it was not a piece of history at all, being as much present in the world of his day as a thousand years earlier and shadowing every human political community throughout any possible future. What it showed men was not how the past once was, but merely what human political authority could amount to.

What such authority could amount to was simple enough: the joining together of the powers of individual human beings to enforce the law of nature and the consequent abandonment of these powers for most purposes by ordinary members of political society. The advantages of this fusion were the greater chance of impartiality in judging and implementing rules of common life, and the improved prospects for peace which such impartiality offers. The hazard of this fusion, a hazard at the forefront of Locke's mind as he wrote, was the huge increase in coercive power that it gave to a political sovereign and the ever present danger that this power too would be abused. Human partiality is central to the human condition. Greater power makes partiality more dangerous; and where greater power is corrupted by flattery and obsequiousness the dangers of partiality in practice become overwhelming. Locke recognized the practical value of great power for human purposes; but he feared it deeply and he thought, as we have every reason still to do, that it can only be trusted when those who hold it see themselves as responsible to (and can be held responsible to) those over whom they exercise it.

Many States of his day, as Locke well knew, were formed by violent conquest. Their political authority, therefore, in no sense rested on the joining together of the powers of their subjects to execute the law of nature. For Locke such States possessed no legitimate political authority. They were structures of force, not of right: not civil societies at all. The relation of a conqueror to the conquered, even after centuries, was a relation not of political authority but of concealed war (T II 192).

In civil societies political authority rests in the last instance on agreement, on consent. Absolute monarchy, by contrast, was inconsistent with civil society (II 90). On any given occasion in an absolute monarchy most of its inhabitants may well have a duty to obey the holder of political power, if what he commands is at the time beneficial or if disobeying him will cause pain and danger to others; but the holder of political power has no right to command his subjects. Only the agreement of adult human beings can give another human being political authority over them. This is a drastic claim; and it raised two principal difficulties for Locke. The first, important in relation to Filmer, was the need to show that such agreements had ever in fact taken place, and, more particularly, that they had done so in England. The second, more striking in the light of modern anarchist criticism of the concept of political authority itself, was to show how every adult member of a legitimate political society could reasonably be supposed to have consented to its political sovereign. In neither case was Locke's answer impressive. The historical challenge to provide instances of such agreement and to indicate when in English history these had occurred, he met simply by evasion. Since all parties to the Exclusion dispute agreed that England was a legitimate State and all paid at least lip-service to the role of English representative institutions in giving their consent to legislation, this was not a costly tactic. The second challenge, to show how each adult in a legitimate State could and did incur clear political duties towards that State, he met more elaborately by distinguishing two kinds of consent: express (overt) and tacit. Express consent made a man a full member of his society for life, with all the rights and duties which followed from such membership. Tacit consent, less intimidatingly, made a man subject to the laws of the country as long as he remained within it, but did not give him either membership of the society or the rights (above all, rights of political choice) which followed from such membership. Express consent explained why members of a legitimate polity had the appropriate range of rights and duties. But it did so by blandly ignoring the fact that virtually no Englishman at the time had voluntarily assumed any such responsibilities at adulthood. Tacit consent reassuringly guaranteed that everyone in England had a duty to obey the law. But it cast very little light on just who amongst his adult male contemporaries Locke considered to be a full member of his society.

In the time of the Exclusion controversy, however, the scope of membership in the political community was not actively at issue, as it had been in the Putney debates within the Parliamentary armies between the Leveller leaders and their generals Cromwell and Henry Ireton in the winter of 1647. Locke's treatment of consent is designed to handle a less ambitious range of questions. Principally it is intended to explain why there can be a fundamental distinction between legitimate and illegitimate political societies, a possibility denied both by Filmer and by Hobbes. Legitimate political societies are societies in which the government has a right to be obeyed. The duties which men owe one another under the law of nature, even in the state of nature, explain quite sufficiently why in a settled political society most men most of the time have a duty to obey their rulers. Locke's theory of consent is not a theory of the political obligations of subjects, of how subjects can have political duties. More particularly it is not a more or less forlorn attempt to prove to the socially disaffected the solid stake which they possess in the preservation of social order. Rather, it is an attempt to explain how rulers (the rulers of civil societies, though not of absolute monarchies) can have rights to political authority.

Locke certainly wrote to proclaim a right of revolution; but he was not in any sense an enemy of political authority. Within its due constitutional limits political authority was an immense human good. Even beyond the legalistic definition of these limits, the royal prerogative could and should be exercised for the public good, despite the letter of the law. If exerted with responsibility and good will, political authority could expect in practice to receive the trust that it deserved. If a narrow constitutionalism is above all an attempt to secure a government of laws, not men, Locke in the last resort set human good intentions above constitutional rigour. In the end all human governments were governments of men (D 122 n. 2). Much of the *Second Treatise* is taken up with constitutional issues, particularly with the connections between private property, popular consent, representative institutions, and the power to make law. It was the vigour of its insistence on the illegitimacy of taxation without representation that nearly a century later so endeared it to the American colonists. But in its central commitments the *Two Treatises*, however skilful its handling of constitutional issues, was not a constitutionalist tract. Instead it proclaimed two intractable rights: the right of a ruler within a legitimate political society to use political power against the law for the public good; and the right of all men to resist the ruler even of a legitimate political society where he grossly abuses his power.

The centrality of trust

At the centre of Locke's conception of government – and catching the ambivalence of this vision – was the idea of trust. Government was a relation between men, between creatures all of whom were capable of deserving trust and any of whom could and sometimes would betray it. Trust was one of the oldest terms in Locke's thinking. The indispensability and the peril of trust were fundamental to human existence. Men, as he wrote in 1659, 'live upon trust'. A few years later, in his lectures, his sharpest criticism of the view that individual interest could be the foundation of the law of nature was that this would not only make such a law self-contradictory, but also make impossible society itself and the trust that was the bond (*vinculum*) of society (LN 213–14). The plainest embodiments of this human need were the actions of swearing and promising. Promises and oaths bound God himself (T I 6). Language might be 'the great Instrument, and common Tye of Society' (E 402): but what enabled it to tie men together in practice was its capacity to express their commitments to one another, the solemn promises, oaths, and undertakings on which their trust in one another necessarily rested and which constituted the bonds (*vincula*) of their common life (LT 134). The menace of atheism (134) was that it removed all force from these undertakings, reducing the law of nature to the contradictory interests of individuals and dissolving the grounds for human trust. Bereft of a concerned Creator and left on their own, men could have no good reason to trust one another and hence no capacity to live in society together. If it were not for human degeneracy (the Fall of Man), men would still belong to a single community (T II 128). To lose sight of their dependence on their Creator would be the final degeneration, disintegrating the many 'smaller and divided associations' of Locke's day into the lonely and distrustful individuals of whom they were composed. In so far as human beings can deserve each other's trust, they help to hold together the community which God intended for them. In so far as they betray each other's trust, they help to promote its disintegration. Holders of political authority, of course, possess this power to sustain or thwart God's purposes in a far more drastic form. Because men are so aware of their need to trust one another and because they sense the aid which this concentrated power to execute the law of nature can offer to their lives, they will on the whole trust their rulers far beyond the latters' deserts. And because peace is so essential to 'the Safety, Ease and Plenty' (II 101) of their lives, it is on balance desirable that they should do so.

Locke does not, like a modern anarchist, distrust political power itself, though he is keenly aware of the dangers which it presents. What he distrusts, rather, is human beings left to their own devices, human beings who no longer grasp their dependence on their divine Creator. For human beings who are still aware of this dependence, the attempt to trust in one another, in rulers as much as in fellow subjects, is a duty under the law of nature. But it is a duty to seek peace, not a duty to deny the lessons of experience. The duty to trust is not a duty to be credulous, perhaps not even a right to be credulous. Even an absolute monarch, in a state of nature with his subjects, is not beyond the reach of human trust. Civil sovereigns are entitled to an ampler trust; and if they deserve it they may be confident of receiving it. But any man, even the sovereign of the most civil of societies, can betray trust. That is just what human life is like. We must try to trust one another, personally as well as politically; but we must all judge, too, when and how far our trust has been betrayed.

Trust may seem a feeble and clumsy concept to put at the centre of an understanding of politics. The connections between Locke's religious views and his sense of the scope of human trustworthiness will not (and should not) endear his estimate of the latter to many today. But, as it worked in his own imagination, the vision of politics and of human life more generally as resting ultimately upon trust was not a superficial view. Its imprecision was a necessary imprecision; and the impossibility of escaping from this imprecision was its central point. Politics is still like this.

The reverse of trust deserved was trust betrayed; and the remedy for the betrayal of trust was the right of revolution. An impartial authority to appeal to on earth was the major benefit that a legitimate political society offered its members. Where it existed, it excluded the state of war between men and removed the need to appeal directly to God's judgement which was intrinsic to this state (T II 21). But impartiality was a human achievement, not a fact of constitutional law. Rulers are real men and women. They hold their authority under law; and entitlement to the obedience of their subjects derives from the impartial administration of this law. Where they act against or outside this law to the harm of their subjects, they become tyrants. Wherever law ends, tyranny begins (II 202). For a ruler in authority to use force against the interests of his subjects and outside the law is to destroy his own authority. He puts himself into a state of war with his injured subjects, and each of these has the same right to resist him as they would have to resist any other unjust aggressor (II 202, 232).

In the England of Locke's day this was a very extreme doctrine; and he went to some pains to play down its practical implications. No ruler who truly means the good of his people will fail to make them feel this (II 209), and no such ruler need fear resistance from his people. Stray acts of tyranny will pass unchallenged, since their victims cannot in practice expect the support of their fellow subjects and cannot hope to challenge the tyrant on their own (II 208, 223, 225). Only a clear threat, actual or potential, to the estates, liberties, and lives (and perhaps also the religion) of the majority (II 209), 'a long train of Actings' (II 220), will bring resistance. But if resistance does come, there is no ambiguity as to who is responsible for its occurrence. To disturb government is a breach of the law of nature; and to rebel without just cause against a legitimate government is to initiate a state of war. (To initiate a state of war is always an unjust act. The only just wars are wars of self-defence.) But when the oppressed people resist tyranny it is not they who disturb government or bring back the state of war. Rebellion is an 'Opposition, not to Persons, but Authority' (II 226). A tyrant has no authority. It is tyrants who are the true rebels. Like any other man who has used the force of war to enforce his ends unjustly upon another, a tyrant has revolted from his own kind 'to that of Beasts by making Force which is theirs, to be his rule of right'. In doing so he has rendered himself 'liable to be destroied by the injur'd person and the rest of mankind, that will joyn with him in the execution of Justice, as any other wild beast, or noxious brute with whom Mankind can have neither Society nor Security' (II 172).

The right to destroy noxious brutes is a right of every human being. But in a legitimate political society even the worst of tyrants cannot be seen simply as vermin. Besides the right to avenge individual injuries, there is also the duty to preserve civil society. Revolution for Locke is not an act of revenge; it is an act of restoration, of the re-creation of a violated political order. In the course of the Exclusion controversy and again in the reign of James II, the King, in Locke's eyes, had become a tyrant and had abused the licence given by his prerogative powers (II 242). Within the English constitution, because the King held part of the power of lawmaking, there was no superior to whom he was obliged to answer. But behind the formalities of the constitution there lay the reality of English society, the 'Body of the People' (II 242, 243). Where a controversy arose between the ruler and a section of his subjects and where the ruler refused to accept the verdict of the representative institutions which expressed the will of his subjects, the proper umpire must be the Body of the People who had first placed their trust in him. The Body of the People can and must judge in their own conscience whether or not they have just cause to appeal to Heaven, to resist their ruler by force (II 163, 243, 21). They have the right and duty to do so because they alone can fuse the right of individual revenge and the responsibility for re-creating political order, the right to destroy those who have betrayed their trust and the duty to restore the trust without which no truly human life is practically possible.

The *Two Treatises* are addressed to the political needs of England, a country in which, through lengthy historical experience, the inhabitants have shown that they form a single body and possess the political capacity to act as such. In England there is an ancient constitution to restore (II Preface). We have no means of knowing how far Locke regarded the inhabitants of countries with less fortunate historical experiences as enjoying the same practical political capacity. Certainly their inhabitants, too, possessed the right individually and collectively to resist unjust force and to avenge the harm which it had inflicted upon them. But where there has never been a legitimate political order to restore, the prospects for uniting revenge and reconstruction are less inviting. Despite its economic, social, and political complexity, an absolute monarchy (and we should remember that Locke had lived for years in France before the time when he was writing) was not a civil society at all. When, in the next century, David Hume set himself to criticize Locke's political theory, no element of it more offended him than this complacent and parochial contrast between England and the absolute monarchies of the Continent. Hume was in some ways an unsympathetic and inaccurate critic of Locke's arguments; and by the end of the 18th century the trajectory of the French Revolution had made it evident that, even on this question, there was more substance to Locke's conceptions than Hume had allowed. But he did see very clearly how closely Locke's view of politics in the *Two*

Treatises depended upon a particular political experience and the culture which this experience had fostered, a community in which a wide range of ordinary citizens held and expected to exercise the right to act politically for themselves. The core of Locke's own understanding of the right to revolution was the right and capacity of such a community to act to preserve itself as a community. He never supposed that a just revenge by itself would suffice to create from nothing a new civil society.

The *Letter on Toleration*

The last major work of political theory which he wrote in the mid-1680s in Holland was less narrowly directed. The *Letter on Toleration* is a simpler as well as a more universal work than the *Two Treatises*. Its arguments do, it is true, depend upon accepting the truth of the Christian religion (or at least of some monotheistic religion in which authentic belief is a precondition for valid religious worship and religious worship is the central duty for man). But within European Christendom the arguments hold, if they hold at all, for every denomination or country. Because the key duty of every man's life is to seek his own salvation (LT 124, 128), and because religious belief and practice are the means by which he must do so, the power of human political authority cannot rightfully extend over either of them. It is the responsibility of political authority to protect civil goods, more particularly the fruits of men's industry and the liberty and bodily strength that are their means of acquiring these (124, 146). The magistrate can have no authority in the care of men's souls. If he judges his actions to be for the public good and his subjects judge the contrary, there can be no judge on earth between them (128) and the verdict must in practice be left to God. Where violent persecution on religious grounds menaces men's properties and lives, the persecuted have every right to repel force with force (146); and they can and will exercise this right. Two main groups are excluded from a right of religious toleration: those whose religious beliefs are directly opposed to the legitimate authority of the magistrate, and those who do not believe in God.

The right to save one's own soul is not a right to attempt to impose a personal political judgement against the civil power. There is no right, as Locke had already insisted in his *Essay* of 1667, to disbelieve in the existence of God, since belief in a God is 'the foundation of all morality' and a man who lacks it is a noxious beast incapable of all society. The use of force against speculative opinions or religious beliefs is unnecessary, since the truth can look after itself and seldom receives much aid from the mighty (122). It is also

11. A hero even to his valet? Locke in Dutch exile in 1685, drawn by his amanuensis and former valet, Sylvanus Brownover.

ineffective since no man can directly choose what he believes or feels. But atheism is not simply a speculative opinion. It is also a ground for limitlessly amoral action. Because the right to toleration depends upon the right and duty of each man to seek his own salvation, it is not a right which any atheist can consistently claim.

The conviction that the truth can look after itself was certainly optimistic. But it was not the foundation of Locke's commitment to toleration. The existence of a God, startlingly, was not a truth that could be left to look after itself. The denial of toleration to atheists, accordingly, however affronting it may be to us today, was fully consistent with Locke's argument. To take away God, even in thought alone, dissolves everything (134). Locke had written the *Letter* late in the winter of 1685, following protracted discussions with his friend Limborch and in the face of Louis XIV's mounting persecution of the Huguenots. He wrote it not for England alone but for a European audience; and it was perhaps to a European audience that it carried most effectively. For Voltaire in the next century the *Letter* was the essence of Locke's politics, a politics wholly in harmony with the message of the great *Essay* and unmistakably relevant to civilized life everywhere on earth. But if its political message was as cosmopolitan as it was clear, it also rested ultimately on a single conviction, the conviction that men have religious duties and can know what these are. It was Locke's struggle to justify this conviction that led to his greatest intellectual achievement. But the struggle itself ended not in triumph but in something very close to surrender.

Chapter 3
Knowledge, belief, and faith

As far as we know, there was no point in Locke's life at which he doubted, simply as a truth of experience, that some men did know their duty to God. But there was also no point in his intellectual life at which he supposed the grounds for this conviction to be clear and easy to explain. As early as 1659, before any of his formal writings, he had set out with vigour and imagination a picture of the relation between men's beliefs and their desires in which reason was seen unblinkingly as the slave of the passions. Instead of austerely controlling men's actions, it served merely as a device for finding grounds for what they already wished to do. Worse still, its failure was not just a failure of control, a moral defect. For the moral failure in its turn both contaminated the entire range of their understanding, and imperilled any solid sense that each man possesses an individual identity of his own (LC I 122–4). These three themes recur throughout his intellectual life, sometimes with more assurance and sometimes with greater pain. The view that many human beliefs deserve blame, that men are in large measure *responsible* for their beliefs, was one of Locke's deepest convictions, but also one which he found acute difficulty in justifying. To be coherent at all, it required a clear conception of how in principle men can remove the contaminations of passion from the operation of their understanding, how they can perceive and comprehend God's world and themselves as these truly are and not as they would prefer them to be. As well as this, it also required a clear conception of each individual man as a being capable of taking responsibility for his own actions. The conceptions of moral agency and of the scope and limits of human understanding were closely linked in Locke's thinking. Where the tension between them became acute, as it did in the years following the publication of the *Essay*, it was the implications of the conception of moral agency that he chose to follow. But of the two, of course, it was the picture of the scope and limits of human understanding, set out in the *Essay*, that Locke himself recognized as his masterpiece; and it has been this that has marked the imagination of posterity.

The first work in which he attempted to explore these themes was a set of lectures at Christ Church, the *Essays on the Law of Nature*. Natural law is decreed by God's will and it can and should be grasped by the light of nature, through the exercise of human reason. Within the order of nature, it shows men what they should and should not do: what this order requires of them as rational agents (LN 110). In the central controversy in Christian ethical theory since the Middle Ages, the dispute between those who saw human obligations as resting fundamentally on the will of God and those who saw them as resting solely on the requirements of reason and the real features of the natural world, Locke's position was equivocal. Clearly he felt (and indeed continued to feel throughout his life) the force of each of these views. But wherever he was compelled to choose between the two (and most conspicuously where he felt that human compliance with the law of nature was importantly in doubt), it was the will of God in which he trusted. In the *Essays* he made little attempt to explore, still less to resolve, the apparent tensions between these views. Nor did he spend much energy in defending the existence, and the binding force, of a law of nature against sceptical objections. (It is instructive, however, that his final response to such doubts was the charge that the absence of a law of nature would make each man the utterly free and supreme arbiter of his own actions (118) – an objection which falls very strangely on the modern ear.)

Instead he concentrated his attention on the question of how exactly men could know what the law was. Four possible ways of knowing are outlined: inscription, tradition, sense-experience, and supernatural, or divine, revelation. The last is discarded (122), not because there is any reason to doubt its occurrence, but because it is clearly not something that men can know merely through their own minds, reason, or sense-experience. (It is, however, to this possibility that Locke returns more than 30 years later in *The Reasonableness of Christianity*.) Inscription is rejected as simply false. If it were true that the law of nature was written in the hearts of all men (140, 144), all would agree in both the moral and the speculative principles which they believed; and the young, the uneducated, and the barbarous would have an especially clear grasp of these principles (138, 140). Tradition is rejected because the moral convictions of different societies differ so drastically. One society's property is another society's theft. One people's lechery is another people's good fellowship or religious worship. In certain circumstances, and in some countries, even murder and suicide can be applauded (166–76). Only the rational interpretation of the experience of the senses survives unscathed. Locke says rather little about how he sees its operation (146–58). But he emphasizes strongly that the main lessons which it offers concern the power and will of God (152–6). He also makes it very clear why he believes that it alone can serve as a foundation for the law of nature. Only a law grounded in the clear working of the human understanding and taking accurate account of the real features of the natural world could have rational authority for human beings as natural creatures. As they actually exist, men's beliefs, as he repeatedly insists, come to them largely from the speech of other men (128, 130, 140–2). The speech of other men is marked by the corruption of human sin. It is only when his beliefs depend upon the workings of his own mind and the lessons of his own experience that a man has good reason to place his trust in them.

The *Essay concerning Human Understanding*

In the *Essay* itself, and more practically in *Some Thoughts concerning Education* and *The Conduct of the Understanding*, Locke attempted to show how men can use their minds to know what they need to know and to believe only what they ought to believe. Because human beings are free, they must think and judge for themselves (E 100, 264). Reason must be their last judge and guide in everything (704). Where reason does not guide their formation, men's opinions are 'but the effects of Chance and Hazard, of a Mind floating at all Adventures, without choice, and without direction' (669). Although it has its own pleasures (6, 43, 233, 259), 'all Reasoning is search, and casting about, and requires Pains and Application' (52). Because it is so easy for men to judge wrongly, and because there is much more falsehood and error amongst men than truth and knowledge (657), all human beings have good reason to 'spend the days of this our Pilgrimage with Industry and Care' (652) in the search for truth. What the *Essay* attempts to offer is practical aid in this search. It does so in two rather different ways. The first is to show how the human understanding works successfully: how it is capable of knowledge and of rational belief, what human beings can know and what they cannot. The second is to explain why on the whole in practice it works so badly. Both these preoccupations were essential to Locke. If human beings could not in principle know what they needed to know, their predicament would place in doubt either the good will or the power of a divine Creator. But if they could not help acting as they did, not only would they be unfree, and hence not responsible for their apparent actions; but God himself would be the cause of all that Locke most loathed in human beings.

Both preoccupations are clearly present in the earliest draft of the *Essay* (EA 142–56). The published text of the first edition devotes much fuller attention to the former. But the balance is partially redressed in Locke's lifetime by a series of amendments, to the second (1694) and fourth editions (1700); in particular by his major change of mind on the nature of free agency, and by the new chapters on enthusiasm and on the association of ideas. (This last chapter was of enormous importance in the history of psychology as a would-be science throughout the 18th and 19th centuries, as well as in the development of utilitarian ethics.) But even after these amendments, the *Essay* very much retained the shape and character of its first published edition; and in this form, the picture of human knowledge and belief that it presents is on the whole an optimistic one. It is optimistic not because it makes extravagant promises of the degree to which human nature can be changed by political design, nor because it exaggerates the extent of human knowledge or minimizes the difficulties which men face in regulating their beliefs in a rational manner, but because it considers the workings of men's minds in such simple, sober, and unpretentious terms. The optimism is more a matter of tone than of content; but as a tone, it proved exceptionally beguiling.

What underlies it, above all, is a remarkable assurance about the scope of possible agreement in human thought.

> I am apt to think, that Men, when they come to examine them, find their simple *Ideas* all generally to agree, though in discourse with one another, they perhaps confound one another with different Names. I imagine, that *Men* who abstract their Thoughts, and do well examine the *Ideas* of their own Minds, cannot much differ in thinking. (E 180: and see LC IV 609)

If men will only use their minds and their senses – the 'inlets' of knowledge – carefully and sincerely, they will find themselves *compelled* to know and believe what they should and thus compelled to agree with those of their fellows who make an equally sober and honest use of their faculties. A key element in achieving and sustaining such agreement is a recognition of the limitations, what Locke himself calls the 'mediocrity', of human understanding. As elsewhere, at the centre of his thinking there lay a fine balance between scepticism and faith.

AN
ESSAY

CONCERNING

Humane Understanding.

In Four BOOKS.

Quam bellum est velle confiteri potius nescire quod nescias, quam ista effutientem nauseare, atque ipsum sibi displicere ! Cic. de Natur. Deor. *l.* 1.

LONDON:

Printed for *Tho. Basset,* and sold by *Edw. Mory*
at the Sign of the *Three Bibles* in St. *Paul's*
Church-Yard. MDCXC.

---

12. Locke's official public intellectual debut, the first edition of the
Essay concerning Human Understanding.

The salience of the faith is hardest to miss when he itemizes what men do in fact know, or sketches how they have good reason to live their lives. The most important single item of possible knowledge is the existence of God: 'we more certainly know that there is a GOD, than that there is any thing else without us' (E 621; and see 619, 628–31, 638). What makes it so important is its immediate and overwhelming implications for how men should live (542, 570, 651). Man's very power to know anything is not something that simply appears from nothing in the course of the history of the world – so that there 'was a time then, when there was no knowing Being, and when Knowledge began to be' (620). Rather, it was a direct gift from an all-knowing God who has existed for all eternity (625). The true ground of morality is 'the Will and Law of a God, who sees men in the dark, has in his Hand Rewards and Punishments, and Power enough to call to account the Proudest Offender' (69).

The nature of moral belief

Locke's view that morality was a science as much open to demonstration as mathematics, forcefully expressed in the *Essay*, caused him much subsequent distress as one friend or enemy after another enquired insistently about his progress towards carrying out the demonstration. There were several reasons for his confidence in the project. Moral ideas were inventions of the human mind, not copies of bits of nature. This contrast has fundamental implications for the character of moral ideas and for how, if at all, these can be known to be valid. It is the foundation in modern philosophical thinking of the presumption of a stark gap between facts about the world (which can potentially be known) and values for human beings (which can merely be embraced or rejected). The distinction between fact and value is both a product of Locke's conception of human knowing and the subversion of his beliefs about human values. Because moral ideas were inventions of the human mind, and because they were marked by words which were also inventions of the human mind, a man could, if only he took the trouble, grasp them perfectly himself and discuss them with other men in a manner which secured an equally perfect understanding on their part.

Much more importantly, human mental invention in the field of morality is not an arbitrary matter. What prevents it from being so, in Locke's view, is the fact that all men can secure, if they will only take the trouble to consider the question, a demonstrative knowledge of the existence of an omnipotent God who prescribes a law to human actions and punishes those which violate it. In the course of their history human communities have invented a wide variety of moral conceptions and adopted extremely diverse moral values. They have also succeeded in some measure in enforcing these values, both through direct coercion and through the subtler pressures of mutual approval or disapproval, the 'law of reputation'. Moral consciousness is not innate in human beings. Indeed, it takes very different forms in different countries. But for Locke, there is a single form which it should take everywhere and always: the form indicated in the Christian revelation and required by the law of nature, a law which men are just as capable of understanding, both extensively and precisely, as they are the truths of mathematics. There is no reason to believe that he ever abandoned this view. But what he clearly did abandon, after a series of abortive attempts to construct a demonstrative scheme of this kind, was the hope that such attempts stood the least chance of affecting how most men chose in practice to behave.

It seems clear from what we know about the *Essay*'s composition that this abandonment represented a major change in intellectual judgement. Indeed there is some reason to believe that it reflected the surrender of one of Locke's two main ambitions in writing the work, and even the disappointment of the initial hope and purpose which first led him to undertake it at all (E 7, 11, 46–7: EA 35–41, 80). But however unwelcome an outcome it may have been, it was not a surprising conclusion to draw from the arguments of the

Essay as a whole. Both knowledge and rational belief are on Locke's account in the last instance compulsive. Faced with the clearly perceived relation between ideas, the direct evidence of their senses, or the plainly apparent balance of probabilities, men cannot but know, sense, or judge as these dictate. Demonstrative ethics would consist of a sequence of relations between ideas which, if considered with care and in good faith, a man or woman could not but see as they are and hence could not deny. In the same way, a man cannot but in the end do what appears to him most desirable, though he certainly can, and often should, check his impulses and force himself to consider carefully and conscientiously whether what he feels immediately drawn to do will in fact be the best action from all points of view. (It is particularly important for him to do this, since absent goods do not catch the attention as insistently as present pains and hence have less purchase on human desires (E 260–1).) In itself human understanding for the most part, and in the most important respects – 'those which concern our Conduct' (46) – works just as it should. But it can do so only if men use it with energy, care, and good intentions. In the case of the practical knowledge of nature, the abuse of the human mind is hardly likely to be deliberate. A careful consideration of the ways in which the mind works when it works successfully can therefore be expected to assist men in future to use their minds more effectively: in scientific and practical enquiry into the character of the natural world, and in pursuit of the conveniences of life. But when it comes to deciding how to live, all men have strong and insistent motives to think less and to do so altogether more evasively. Not only do they have such motives but, as Locke was at pains to insist, most men in fact succumb to them with rather little resistance. Instead of living their lives in the light of divine threats of infinite and eternal pain (74–5, 255, 273–4, 277, 281–2), many even in civilized countries live as though they were atheists (88). All men are 'liable to Errour, and most Men are in many points, by Passion or Interest, under Temptation to it' (718). To improve men's moral conduct, what is most urgently required is not greater intellectual clarity but more effective imaginative aid in resistance to temptation. (Hence

Locke's decision within a few years of the *Essay*'s first publication to supplement it with a further work, *The Reasonableness of Christianity*, which set out what he took to be a particularly clear, simple, and directive version of Christian belief.)

This shift of attention, followed as it was by the meticulous paraphrasing of St Paul's *Epistles* (on which Locke laboured almost till his death), is profoundly revealing. What it underlines is the close dependence of his conception of the good life for man on the presumption of a God who sees men in the dark, cares how they choose to act, and punishes them after death for acting against his law. Two of the most important and impressive additions to the *Essay*, the altered treatment of free agency and the wholly new chapter on identity, are centrally concerned with the question of how divine punishment can make sense and be just (E 270–1, 340–6, and 717). At no point was Locke prepared to contemplate a conscious preference of faith to the conclusions of reason (667–8, 687–96, 698, 705). Even after writing the *Reasonableness*, he remained confident that the existence of a deity of the required kind could be demonstrated and that it therefore could and should be regarded as a conclusion of reason (LC VI 243–5, 386–91, 596, 630, 788–91). It is easy to see why this judgement was so crucial if we consider in its absence the implications of some of the *Essay*'s other main lines of thought.

The natural condition of man is not a placid one.

> We are seldom at our ease, and free enough from the sollicitation of our natural or adopted desires, but a constant succession of *uneasinesses* out of that stock, which natural wants, or acquired habits have heaped up, take the *will* in their turns; and no sooner is one action dispatch'd, which by such a determination of the *will* we are set upon, but another *uneasiness* is ready to set us on work. (E 262)

In the world, men are 'beset with sundry *uneasinesses*' and 'distracted with different *desires*' (257). Pain and pleasure, good and evil, move men's desires and do so by entering into their conception of happiness (258–9). All men constantly pursue happiness and desire anything which they see as making part of it. This is not a matter of choice. They cannot choose not to pursue happiness. But this does not in any way diminish their responsibility for what they choose to do. God himself 'is under the necessity of being Happy'; and it is the point of human liberty that men should have the power and responsibility to judge for themselves what really is good (264–5). Just as men's tastes in food differ – some loving lobster and cheese but others loathing them – so do their tastes in those broader and more diverse conceptions of pleasure which depend on the mind. Some value riches; others bodily delights; others virtue; and others contemplation. Since pleasure is a matter of taste, it is absurd to deny that men's happiness in this world will take very different forms.

> If therefore Men in this Life only have hope; if in this Life they can only enjoy, 'tis not strange, nor unreasonable, that they should seek their Happiness by avoiding all things, that disease them here, and by pursuing all that delight them ... For if there be no Prospect beyond the Grave, the inference is certainly right, *Let us eat and drink*, let us enjoy what we delight in, *for tomorrow we shall die* ... Men may chuse different things, and yet all chuse right, supposing them only like a Company of poor insects, whereof some are Bees, delighted with Flowers, and their sweetness; others, Beetles, delighted with other kind of Viands; which having enjoyed for a season, they should cease to be, and exist no more for ever. (E 269–70)

Occasionally Locke does attempt to argue that even in this life the rewards of virtue exceed those of vice (281–2). But the main weight of his judgement clearly falls against this view (W III 93). If happiness depends solely upon individual taste and taste itself is beyond criticism, human appetites can be restrained only by human threats – psychological, moral, and physical. Even within this world, the restraint of men's appetites will be indispensable if society is to remain possible. 'Principles of Actions indeed there are lodged in Men's Appetites, but these are so far from being innate Moral Principles, that if they were left to their full swing, they would carry Men to the over-turning of all Morality' (E 75). If men's nature compelled them to see their moral predicaments as Locke saw these – 'a Pleasure tempting, and the Hand of the Almighty visibly held up, and prepared to take Vengeance' (74) – most of them would certainly alter their habitual choices. But if men's reason came to question and reject the reality of this threat, their habitual choices might prove quite well considered, indeed might compare favourably with those of Locke himself. The key judgement for Locke is that a man can deserve punishment for an evil action because this action demonstrates that he has 'vitiated his own Palate' (271). It depends for its coherence, as well as its force, on there being a valid standard for human conduct independent of what men happen to find attractive.

The nature of knowledge

Most of the *Essay* is not directly concerned with moral questions. But even in the parts of the book which set out his theory of how men can know about nature, Locke's conception of the relations between God and man often plays an important role. It does so, not by qualifying the conclusions of the ambitious and impressively systematic theory which he developed, still less by questioning the value of any such theory, but rather by setting it in a congenial imaginative frame. In some respects he sees the scope of human knowledge as sharply restricted. But within this scope, he has no doubt whatever of its reality as knowledge. Although he explicitly denies that knowledge enters history along with the human race, he thinks of knowledge as something of which we may be quite certain that men are naturally capable. God – and even angels and other spirits – may know vastly more and know it more directly (M 52). All men may be mistaken in many of their beliefs (though he doubted in fact if the beliefs which they actually possess are often as absurd as much of what they are induced to say that they believe (E 719)). But any human being whose wits are sufficiently in order to consider the question may be perfectly confident, may *know*, that he or she *can* know.

Locke's theory covers many of the great issues of philosophy: the relation of human thought and experience to their objects, how words get and retain their meanings, how men perceive, how human knowing and understanding operate. It is, as he makes very clear, not intended as a scientific theory: a theory, for example, about how exactly in human sight material objects can exercise the power to modify men's minds (M 10), or of why exactly parts of nature act upon other parts just as we observe them to do. On these questions Locke was highly sceptical whether men's natural faculties equipped them to understand very profoundly and precisely: sometimes too sceptical, as it has turned out. But by contrast with these piously affirmed limitations, he believed firmly that men can understand clearly how to distinguish what they can hope to know from what they cannot. More importantly still, he was equally sure that if they applied this understanding in actually using their minds in real life, they could be confident not merely of learning much practically useful information and of greatly extending their scientific understanding of nature, but also of seeing more clearly how they ought to conduct themselves as moral agents. Instead of letting loose their thoughts 'into the vast Ocean of *Being*' (E 47), men would be better advised to consider soberly the capacities of their own understanding and to direct their thought and action accordingly (46).

The *Essay* itself promises to 'consider the discerning Faculties of a Man, as they are employ'd about the Objects, which they have to do with'. Through 'this Historical, plain Method' it aspires to give an 'Account of the Ways, whereby our Understandings come to attain those Notions of Things we have' (44). Its first book attacks the doctrine of innate ideas, ideas with which human beings are born. The view that men do have innate moral and religious ideas Locke had already rejected, as we have seen, in his *Essays on the Law of Nature*. Given the variety of moral values and religious beliefs in different societies of which he was aware, he had no difficulty in making this view appear extremely foolish. This mockery caused grave offence amongst the Anglican clergy of the day and was an important source of Locke's reputation as a propagator of irreligious opinions. More important for the *Essay* as a whole was his rejection of the view, held for example by Descartes, that man's capacity to understand nature also rested upon the innate knowledge of a number of maxims of reason, such as 'What is, is' (48–65). Since most men (and virtually all small children) are quite unaware of any such maxims, it is absurd to attribute knowledge of these to them. The way in which men come to understand the truth of such maxims is through experiencing particular objects. While it is true that they depend for this understanding on the exercise of their rational faculties, this in no sense makes knowledge of the maxims themselves innate.

The remaining three books of the *Essay* set out Locke's own positive theory of how men can know and of how they can form beliefs which it is rational for them to believe. The first develops his account of the nature of ideas, the sole immediate objects of human thought and therefore the only objects about which human knowledge is 'conversant' (525). (By an 'idea' Locke meant merely 'whatsoever is the Object of the Understanding when a Man thinks' (47).) The second considers the nature of words, and of language in general, while the third summarizes the implications of the first two in a bold discussion of the nature of human knowledge. Knowledge itself is a form of perception: the perception of the '*connexion and agreement, or disagreement and repugnancy of any of our Ideas*' (525). What men immediately perceive, and even what they immediately reason about, are always particular ideas existing in their own minds. Any true general conclusions at which they arrive apply only in so far as other particular relations in nature, or in the thought of other men, correspond to them (680–1). Ideas themselves are all either simple or complex. If simple, they derive directly from the senses (310–12), the inlets of knowledge. If complex, they are formed by the voluntary mental union (163) of simple ideas. All human knowledge is founded in and ultimately derived from experience; either from the observation of perceivable objects in the world, or from the inspection and assessment of the workings of men's own minds (106). Men can think, know, and judge for themselves, and must do so since they cannot in the end trust others to do so for them (100–1, 7, 264). The minds of children at birth are like white paper (81, 104). Although at first they are marked plainly by the purely natural impact of particular ideas through the senses, they are also speedily defaced by the often superstitious and irrational teaching of adults (81–4, 394–401). Once so defaced, since custom is a greater power than nature (82), only a lifetime's unrelenting effort, fired by a genuine love for truth itself (697), can do much to repair the damage.

One of the main ways in which human understanding undergoes this corruption is through the words in which men express their thoughts. The systematic discussion of language in the third book came, as Locke himself acknowledges (401, 437, 488), as something of an afterthought. But he had no doubts as to its practical importance: 'The greatest part of the Questions and Controversies that perplex Mankind depending on the doubtful and uncertain use of Words' (13). Since most men most of the time think in words, and since general truths are almost always expressed in words (579), confusion or unnecessary vagueness in the use of words can do immense harm (488–9). Because words 'interpose themselves so much between our Understandings, and the Truth', their obscurity and disorder can 'cast a mist before our Eyes' (488). This effect is particularly disastrous in law, divinity, and moral argument (433, 480, 492, 496).

This insistence on the significance of verbal clarity, the emphasis which he lays on the predominant role of the senses in furnishing men with knowledge of nature, and his conception of the infant mind as blank paper on which experience writes are perhaps the most optimistic of Locke's themes in the *Essay*. The first two still meet with some modern philosophical approval; and all three were important in shaping Locke's image as provider of the philosophical basis for Enlightenment optimism. By contrast, his stress on the power of custom, on the elaborate and treacherous processes through which men form, modify, and protect their beliefs, and on the unedifying character of most men's worldly desires (67, 662) suggests decidedly more pessimistic conclusions. Certainly, it offers no encouragement whatsoever for the more extreme Enlightenment hopes of reforming human nature *en masse* through political control of the environment in which individuals develop. This is especially important because of the close links which Locke himself saw between men's grounds for trusting their senses and the force of their worldly desires. In the last resort he rejected sceptical doubts as to whether our senses really do deliver us any knowledge at all, on two very different grounds. His own conception of how they do so can be considered shortly. But the grounds for rejecting scepticism must first be underlined.

One ground, a partial echo of Descartes, is simple, devout, and unlikely to impress a secular audience: that a good Creator would not have endowed men with senses which systematically deceive them (E 375, 302, 624–5, 631; M 10). But the second is far more complicated and requires no devotion whatsoever. Not only does the evidence of each sense support its own veracity through time. It also supports that of the others. Trust in the senses is so indispensable for practical life and so directly linked to the overwhelmingly powerful stimuli of pleasure and pain – 'the hinges on which our Passions turn' (E 229, 128–30, 254–80, 631, 633–4) – that Locke cannot believe that any human being could sincerely doubt the validity of sense-experience, let alone live as though he supposed it illusory. Whatever the force of particular arguments in its favour, sceptical doubt in practice can only be trivial because the senses play such a central role in how men adapt themselves to and control nature. Because he held such a vivid conception of the demands of virtue (LC I 123) and the seductions of vice, and because belief in God was so essential to sustaining this conception, Locke himself drew no strong implications from this relation between sense and desire. For him, as for Nietzsche nearly two centuries later, if God did not exist, man 'could have no law but his own will, no end but himself. He would be a god to himself, and the satisfaction of his own will the sole measure and end of all his actions' (D 1). The fundamental choice for man would be the choice of what sort of creature to become. But for those (like Jeremy Bentham) whose imaginations were less captivated by virtue, honour, and their repressive demands, the myriad links between sense and desire would in due course suggest a more comfortable and worldly style of life. Locke himself was a utilitarian only in the light of a world to come. But it is easy to see how less devout minds could base an entirely secular utilitarianism on his conception of the human understanding. Whatever his own philosophical judgement of how men who had lost a faith in God would have good reason to live, it is also easy to see how, under these circumstances, Locke would expect them in practice to choose to live. Given the history of religious belief in Western Europe since his death, it is hard to imagine that the corresponding history of moral belief and sentiment would have come to him as much of a surprise.

The varieties of knowledge

In the *Epistle to the Reader* which prefaces the *Essay*, Locke expresses the ambition to serve the master builders of 17th-century natural science – Boyle, Huygens, and Newton – as a mere under-labourer 'removing some of the Rubbish, that lies in the way to Knowledge' (E 9–10). The rubbish is to be removed in two main ways, one negative and the other positive. In the understanding of nature the inventive powers of reason must be restrained sharply in favour of a trust in the less fanciful testimony of the senses. Men cannot hope to understand the workings of nature with the clarity with which they understand, for example, algebra. But by understanding how their minds operate in the acquisition of knowledge, by careful observation of nature and equally careful expression of the results of such observation (476–7, 484, 501), they can hope to extend their understanding greatly. The natural tendency of the human mind is towards knowledge (385). One reason why a comprehensive scepticism is so absurd is that the contrast between truth and illusion which it draws depends upon the very capacity to distinguish which it denies: 'we cannot act any thing, but by our Faculties; nor talk of Knowledge it self, but by the help of those Faculties, which are fitted to apprehend even what Knowledge is' (631).

Men have three principal types of knowledge: intuitive, demonstrative, and sensitive. (The status of memory is a little unclear.) Of these, intuition is the most certain because it is the least avoidable. God's knowledge is intuitive. He sees everything at once and hence has no need, as men do, to reason (M 52). The main truth which men know intuitively is their own existence: this they cannot doubt. Valid demonstration is just as definitely knowledge as is intuition. But, since it necessarily involves relations between several different ideas, it is 'painful, uncertain and limited' (52) in comparison with intuition; and men can be, and often are, mistaken in supposing themselves to have achieved it. Mathematical knowledge is demonstrative. But the most important truth which men can know demonstratively is the existence of God. Sensitive knowledge is caused by the action of objects in the world upon human senses (E 630–8). We do not know exactly how it is caused (M 10). But this ignorance does not make it any less certain (E 630). Seeing white paper as one writes on it, it is as impossible to doubt the colour seen or the real existence of the paper as it is to doubt the act of writing or the movement of one's hand: 'a Certainty as great, as humane Nature is capable of, concerning the Existence of any thing, but a Man's self alone, and of GOD' (631). Sensitive knowledge fully *'deserves the name of Knowledge'* (631). It extends *'as far as the present Testimony of our Senses*, employ'd about particular Objects, that do then affect them, *and no farther'* (635); with the crucial exception that our memories, when accurate, give us knowledge of the past existence of some things of which our senses once assured us (636).

Memory is an important supplement to demonstrative as well as to sensitive knowledge. Without it, no general truths in mathematics could be known; nor could we possess even 'habitual' knowledge of the truth of any demonstrations we had completed in the past unless we saw perfectly in the present just how to repeat them; nor could Newton, for example, be said to know what he had demonstrated in his *Principia* except when he held its full chain of reasoning 'in actual view' (528–30).

13. Locke as ghostly enemy of Postmodernism: the conviction that truth is opposite to falsehood, that it may be found and is worth the seeking.

This conception of knowledge has been criticized from many angles. Few modern philosophers would accept Locke's demonstration of God's existence. But much the most important and widespread attack has been levelled at his analysis of sensitive knowledge. A succession of able critics of widely varying views, from Berkeley, Thomas Reid, and Kant to the present day, have questioned the compatibility of the two main components of his view: that the senses give men knowledge of the external world, and that all knowledge consists of mental acquaintance with ideas. Locke's doctrine is in fact a complicated and subtle one; and many of the objections which have been raised against it certainly miss the mark. He definitely does hold that simple ideas of natural objects correspond in some strong fashion to the way natural objects actually are: namely, by giving men knowledge of their qualities. In doing so, such ideas differ radically from, for instance, moral conceptions, which do not involve the attempt to match some pre-existing 'archetype' outside the human mind. He also definitely holds an essentially causal theory of perception: that the way in which the senses furnish us with knowledge of nature is by the qualities of objects causing ideas in our minds. He also plainly imagines the causal mechanisms in question very much in the 17th-century scientific idiom of matter and motion (M 10): it is plain that 'Motion has to do in the producing of them: And Motion so modified is appointed to be the cause of our having them.' But he did not suppose for a moment that human beings in his day possessed any clear understanding of how exactly this causality works, and he plainly doubted that their senses were acute enough to equip them to understand it even in principle. Yet, although his theory was in this way more elaborate and sceptical than is sometimes recognized, it does have important weaknesses. It is reasonable to insist that all knowing involves mental action and some element of consciousness. It remains a plausible claim, at least in relation to the external world, that 'since the Things, the Mind contemplates, are none of them, besides it self, present to the Understanding, 'tis necessary that something else, as a Sign or Representation of the thing it considers, should be present to it:

And these are Ideas' (720–1). But the view that the whole of man's capacity to know can be adequately explained as the acquisition and recombination of simple ideas, furnished by the individual senses or by reflection, remains unconvincing.

On this basis, nevertheless, Locke was able to erect an impressive analysis of natural philosophy: 'The Knowledge of Things, as they are in their own proper Beings, their Constitutions, Properties, and Operations' (720). It was an account which recognized the potential deceptions of the senses and of memory, without succumbing to a comprehensive scepticism. It distinguished firmly, if not always very clearly, between those 'primary' qualities of nature (such as shape) which exist in bodies quite independently of human or other observers and the 'secondary' qualities (like colour) which depend in part upon the perceptual powers of an observer. Men perceive a solid cube as such because, whether they inspect it or not, that is simply the way it is. But they perceive a rose as red because when they see it in daylight its physical properties happen to cause them so to perceive it. All simple ideas are caused by the 'qualities' of objects by means which we do not and probably cannot understand. But unlike secondary qualities, primary qualities in no sense depend upon the relation between human beings and external objects. It is natural for men to think of both sorts of qualities as simply existing in external objects. But only in the case of primary qualities is this natural belief wholly valid.

Knowledge of nature is confined to simple ideas of sensation, perceived in the present or recalled to the mind by memory. But, of course, men's belief about nature extends vastly beyond this. It is founded principally on judgements of probability, based on elaborate comparisons between, and combinations of, simple ideas. Accordingly, it is not a form of knowing about nature, but a form of more or less well-considered guessing about this. Over most of the more important issues in their lives men cannot truly know what to do or what is the case. All they can do is to judge these as prudently as possible. But this they certainly must do. To insist on knowledge in practical questions where it cannot be had would be self-destructive. It would incapacitate men from taking any action at all and bring their lives to a nervous halt. No general truths about nature can be known; and therefore there can in the strict sense be no *science* of nature. Men are entirely correct to believe that they know their simple ideas of sensation and reflection to match reality, the way the world is, and the way they are themselves. But when they attempt to understand themselves and nature, the complex ideas which they fashion in their minds out of these simple materials cannot be known to match reality. Instead, what human beings are compelled to do is to judge whether reality matches their own complex ideas. If they judge attentively and prudently this will serve very adequately for all practical purposes. What God requires of them they cannot afford not to know. But to deal effectively with nature does not demand knowledge. It merely demands skilful guessing.

To possess a true science of external nature, men would need to have sensitive knowledge of general truths about its workings. They would need to be able literally to see how all natural effects are caused. God himself certainly possesses this power of direct vision. It is even possible that angels too, if to a lesser degree, may be able to perceive some of nature's workings directly. But human beings, because of the limitations of their senses, must depend for their understanding of nature quite largely on the self-conscious control of their own conceptions and classifications. If they cannot know general truths about nature, they have the most practical of motives for attempting to form valid general beliefs about its workings. To increase the probability of success in this venture, they must attend particularly to the ways in which they form their own complex ideas and in which they employ the words with which they name these ideas. Simple ideas are natural signs of qualities of natural objects; and words are human signs for ideas in the mind. Simple ideas are entirely involuntary, words wholly voluntary. Standing between these two, complex ideas can be subjected to deliberate regulation by the mind but depend for their materials wholly upon the involuntary deliverance of the senses. Extreme mental and verbal self-consciousness is required for men to secure the fullest control of the conduct of their own understandings. Systematic scientific research and philosophical discourse are the public and practical expressions of a form of mental care and responsibility that all men, within the limits of their social opportunities, have the duty to undertake.

Scientific research does not in Locke's view yield knowledge; and hence for him does not deserve the name of science. But it certainly does enable men to improve their understanding of nature. In the work of his admired contemporaries Boyle, Newton, and other leading lights of the Royal Society, scientific research had recently made great strides. It is not clear how far Locke himself expected this specialized, systematic, and highly theoretical enquiry into the natural world by itself to increase man's control over nature or to enhance his enjoyment of life in the world. (In the field of medicine, of course, he hoped for some immediate worldly benefits; but he clearly did not anticipate a transformation of man's capacity to control disease or alleviate pain.) Yet, whatever its distinct contribution proved to be, he clearly did see scientific research as a natural extension of the active and practical effort to understand and control nature which distinguished 'polished' from 'rude' nations and made life in the former, in his view, so much more enjoyable than it was in the latter (646–7).

Perhaps the most impressive feature of this understanding of natural science was its explanation of the limits of men's natural knowledge. In some ways, to be sure, Locke plainly misjudged these limits, seeing a larger gap between human classification and the workings of nature than the subsequent history of chemistry, or even biology, has proved to justify. But the balance between confidence in the explanatory power of the mechanical model and conviction that men cannot directly know the workings of nature still seems well judged. Modern philosophers of natural science have very different sciences to consider, some with awesome practical effects. They share few of Locke's assumptions, or even interests. Unlike Locke, also, they do not think of knowledge as a form of vision and do not contrast the limitations of man's knowledge of nature with the supposedly perfect vision of an omniscient God. But they too, for the most part, for all their disagreements, put such confidence as they can muster largely in the direct deliverances of the senses and in the explanatory power of models; and they too would deny that human beings can know just why nature works as it does. Natural science, accordingly, is not so much a form of knowledge (as Locke understood this) but, rather, a peculiarly complicated and cunning form of belief – a matter of judgement (or guessing), not of direct vision.

Locke does not doubt that something causes nature to work in every detail just as it does. Objects have qualities and human beings know of their existence because these qualities affect their senses in particular ways. But, unlike Aristotle, he doubted whether nature itself was divided up into distinct kinds of things, with clear boundaries between them; he was confident that human beings could not know exactly how it is divided; and he was quite certain that human beings cannot know about it by knowing precisely how it is divided. However nature itself is divided up – whether it forms a blurred continuum or is made up of a multiplicity of entirely distinct kinds of things – it causes men to see it just as they do; and God can see clearly how and why it does so. But all that men can do is to assemble together their own simple ideas with care and accuracy and to use the verbal signs which refer to these assemblages with equal care and accuracy. What men can know about nature (apart from the simple ideas of sensation and reflection) is how exactly they themselves conceive it. They cannot know in general what they are thinking or talking about. They cannot, except at a particular moment, know how it truly is.

With ideas that shape action – and especially with moral ideas – the position is very different. Here there is no gap between what men think about and what really is the case. It is easy to be confused about moral issues since there is no palpable external standard, given by the senses, which men must seek to match and with which their ideas can readily be compared. But the moral ideas which men consider simply are the realities about which they are attempting to think. Because there is no gap in this sense between what Locke calls their 'nominal essence' and their 'real essence', ideas about morality can be understood with a clarity which ideas about nature necessarily lack. This is why Locke supposed that morality could be demonstrated, and continued to suppose so long after he had abandoned the attempt to demonstrate it himself.

What made moral conceptions potentially so clear (and moral misunderstanding so likely in practice) was the absence of a given world for them to match. Unsurprisingly, however, this very absence made them vulnerable in quite another way. All men, as we have seen, have powerful internal principles of action which impel them to act in a manner wholly contrary to Locke's own moral beliefs. Human societies are possible because they restrain these motives by the contrary pressure of approval and disapproval and by effective threats of legal punishment. Both of these are simply practical obstacles to an individual's pursuit of pleasure. In themselves they can give no man a reason for wishing to act morally, or for choosing to do so where he is confident of avoiding in practice the threats which they level at him. Hence the decisive importance for Locke's conception of morality of a threat which no one can rationally hope to avoid, the punishments of a God 'who sees Men in the dark'. This dependence is set out with particular clarity in an uncompleted manuscript, 'Of Ethics in General', perhaps intended as the final chapter of the *Essay* (LN 11). In face of this dependence, the *Essay* as a whole shows one glaring defect. The demonstrative argument for God's existence which it offers goes no distance at all towards establishing the reality of a God concerned to punish or save human beings. The unmistakably Christian conception of a God on which Locke's moral convictions rested could be vindicated only by an appeal to revelation. (Fortunately, God's law of nature and his revealed will were necessarily identical and offered 'the only true touch-stone of *moral Rectitude*' (E 352).)

Faith

In his last major work, accordingly, Locke turned firmly to
revelation. He did so in part to proclaim, as its title declares, *The
Reasonableness of Christianity as delivered in the Scriptures.* (It is
reason which must judge whether a particular message is or is not a
revelation from God and which must interpret precisely what it
means.) But he did so more urgently because it was only by means
of the Christian revelation that he retained the confidence that
men's moral duties were effectively 'made known to all mankind'.
Natural law in its full extent had never been demonstrated by
anyone (R 89), and by 1694 Locke had abandoned hope of
demonstrating it himself (LC IV 768, 786). But God had shown
all men how he wished them to live by proclaiming to them the
law of faith through the Messiah Jesus. The close correspondence
between the Messianic prophecies of the Old Testament and the
events of the life of Jesus, together with the miracles which he
performed, gave to his disciples a revealed knowledge that he
was the Messiah. Jesus himself proclaimed the law of faith,
demanding obedience and promising salvation in return
(R 71–5; W III 466).

Nearly 17 centuries later, men cannot expect the same direct
compulsion to believe that the disciples enjoyed, since traditional
revelation depends on historical reasoning and not on direct
experience (E 664, 690–1). But if they consider the evidence and
open their hearts, faith will not be denied to them. The faith that
Jesus was the Messiah, and a genuine effort to obey his law, will
together be sufficient to save them. Faith is a form of trust, not
against reason, but beyond reason. It demands effort (which is why
infidelity can be a sin). But it makes truly open to every man the
opportunity to live a good life.

This is not an inspiring conclusion to a philosophical quest that had
covered three and a half decades. There is no reason to believe that
Locke himself regarded it with enthusiasm; and he would scarcely

THE
REASONABLENESS
OF
Christianity,

As delivered in the

SCRIPTURES.

LONDON:

Printed for *Awnsham* and *John Churchil*, at the *Black Swan* in *Pater-Noster-Row.* 1 6 9 5.

14. The step backwards to faith – that Jesus was the Messiah. Not, of course, a new conviction for Locke, but a quite new salience to the conviction.

have been happy to espouse it from the outset. It had, moreover, a number of distressing implications. It meant, for example, that men, by Locke's own criterion and because of the limitations of their own natural abilities, cannot, and do not have the opportunity to, *know* how to live. Judgement and faith may be sufficient for salvation. But what they offer does not amount to a form of knowledge. Moreover, the fate of all those human beings who had not been fortunate enough to receive the good news of the Christian revelation was hard, on this view, to reconcile both with Locke's conception of man's place in nature and with his understanding of the power and benevolence of God.

But, however discouraging an outcome this must have been for Locke himself, it does serve to illuminate some of the key constraints on his imagination. Judgement and faith together could give men sufficient reason to live as he supposed that they ought. In the last instance, it was more important to him that they should have sufficient reason to live in this way than that they should possess the power to know how to live. Genuine knowledge of morality, accordingly, turns out in practice to be as much beyond men's own reach as a true science of nature. What replaces it in the real lives of men, as Locke imagined these, is a combination of judgement with trust in divine benevolence. His picture of men's powers to know about nature – as modest natural abilities – is contrasted with a picture of God's power to know about nature. In the face of these modest natural abilities, sceptical doubt appears strained and silly because, unlike them, it can play no part in meeting the practical demands of day-to-day life. In a sense (and here Locke's profound engagement with the philosophy of Descartes gave him some real insight), the force of scepticism comes largely from an implicit contrast between the modest ability to understand nature which men palpably do possess and a form of understanding – clear, distinct, unchallengeable, and final – which they might in faith be led to attribute to God, but which they themselves certainly cannot attain. From Locke's point of view, that is to say, it comes from the presumptuous demand that men should be able to understand nature as clearly as God does.

With the faltering of trust in the existence of a God, both natural knowledge and morality inevitably look very different from the way that Locke saw them. In a godless world the limits of scepticism were certain to prove (and have proven) far harder to draw.

Conclusion

In January 1698, in a letter to his friend William Molyneux, Locke summed up the convictions of a lifetime.

> If I could think that discourses and arguments to the understanding were like the several sorts of cates [sc. foodstuffs] to different palates and stomachs, some nauseous and destructive to one, which are pleasant and restorative to another; I should no more think of books and study, and should think my time better imploy'd at push-pin than in reading or writing. But I am convinc'd of the contrary: I know there is truth opposite to falsehood, that it may be found if people will, and is worth the seeking, and is not only the most valuable, but the pleasantest thing in the world. (LC VI 294–5)

That the truth is independent of human desires and tastes, and that at least part of it lies within the reach of human understanding, is a simple and widespread conviction. But it is not an easy conviction to explain and justify in any great depth. For Locke, the task of a philosopher was to provide just such an explanation and defence. Many modern philosophers doubt whether any such defence can be constructed. Even amongst those who believe that it might, few see Locke's own attempt as especially successful.

There is no reason to quarrel with this verdict. What distinguishes Locke from the great majority of philosophers is not the cogency

15. An old, sick and immensely distinguished man: Locke in the final year of his life.

today of his arguments as a whole. Rather, it is the profundity with which he understood the bearing of philosophy on how men have good reason to live their lives. If truth does in the end depend upon human desire, and if men have no end but their own wills, then the life which Locke himself lived was a ludicrous exercise in self-denial. Nearly three centuries later, the same is still likely to be true of many aspects of our own lives. The idea that whether or not our lives make sense might depend upon the deliberations of university departments of philosophy is at first sight mildly comic. But in the last instance the joke, as Locke saw, is on us. Once we have lost the religious guarantee that reason, 'the candle of the Lord', shines bright enough for all our purposes, we have no conclusive reason to expect it to shine bright enough for any. And once we can no longer see our purposes as authoritatively assigned to us from outside our selves, it becomes very hard to judge just which purposes we have good reason to consider as (or to make) our own.

In the face of these two hazards, the instability of human belief in its entirety and the obscurity of how we do have good reason to live our lives, Locke's philosophy offers us more illumination on the first than on the second. This is certainly not what he would have wished, but it is easy enough to explain. Many philosophers today, unsurprisingly, share his belief that truths about nature and about complex inventions of the human mind, like mathematics and logic, are independent of human desire. But for Locke the central truths about how men have good reason to live are just as independent of what at a particular time they happen consciously to desire. Few today share this belief with any confidence; and perhaps no one today has much idea of how to defend it. But some still live (and many more attempt intermittently to live) as though it were in fact true. As Coleridge, a savage critic of Locke's ethics, put it a century and three-quarters ago: 'Almost all men nowadays act and feel more nobly than they think.'

The view that the game of push-pin, if men happen to enjoy it as much, is just as good as poetry is a slogan of the most influential modern theory of human good, the utilitarianism of Jeremy Bentham. What led Locke to reject it is not the equally utilitarian (and singularly unconvincing) claim that truth is the pleasantest thing in the world, but the more fundamental conviction that truth is different from falsehood, that it can be found and is worth the seeking, and that when it is found it will tell man clearly how to live. It was in this conviction that he placed his trust and lived his life. Because of it, he still offers to us across the centuries the example of a lifetime of intellectual courage. It may well be that he was wrong to trust it. And if he was, we can hardly rely on his thinking to steady our own nerves. But what is certain is that we too shall need such intellectual courage every bit as urgently as he did.

References

The manuscript by Sydenham quoted on p. 10 is from Kenneth Dewhurst, *John Locke, Physician and Philosopher: A Medical Biography* (Wellcome Historical Medical Library, 1963). Henry Ireton's question to the Leveller leaders in the Putney debates quoted on p. 43 is taken from A. S. P. Woodhouse (ed.), *Puritanism and Liberty* (J. M. Dent & Son, 1938). Coleridge's comment cited on p. 97 comes from Kathleen Coburn (ed.), *The Notebooks of Samuel Taylor Coleridge*, ii. *1804–1808* (New York, 1961), entry 2627.

Further reading

Full bibliographical details of the editions of Locke's works that have been used in references are given in the list of abbreviations at the beginning of the book.

The Clarendon Press is at present engaged in publishing an edition of all Locke's published writings and many of his unpublished manuscripts. The *Essay concerning Human Understanding* and (thus far) eight volumes of his *Correspondence* were the first to appear, superlatively edited by Peter Nidditch and E. S. de Beer respectively. A single volume of *Selected Correspondence*, edited by Mark Goldie (Oxford University Press), now makes some of the vividness and fascination of the full *Correspondence* accessible to a wider readership. A final volume, along with a full index to the *Correspondence* as a whole, will be issued shortly. These two works have since been joined by A *Paraphrase and Notes on the Epistles of St Paul* (ed. Arthur A. Wainwright, 2 vols., 1987), *Some Thoughts on Education* (ed. John W. & Jean S. Yolton, 1989), *Drafts for the Essay concerning Human Understanding and other Philosophical Writings* (ed. Peter H. Nidditch and G. A. J. Rogers, 1990), *Locke on Money* (2 vols., ed. Patrick Hyde Kelly, 1991), and *The Reasonableness of Christianity* (ed. John Higgins-Biddle, 1999). There are also excellent modern editions of the Two *Treatises of Government* (ed. Peter Laslett, Cambridge University Press, 2nd edn., 1988), *Two Tracts on Government* (ed. Philip Abrams, Cambridge University Press, 1968), *Essays on the Law of Nature* (ed. W. von Leyden, Clarendon Press,

1954), and a somewhat less satisfactory edition of the *Letter on Toleration* (ed. R. Klibansky and J. W. Gough, Clarendon Press, 1967). There are also very useful selections across the range of Locke's views about politics in David Wootton's *Political Writings of John Locke* (Penguin, 1993), a full and careful presentation of many of his incidental writings on politics in Locke, *Political Essays*, ed. Mark Goldie (Cambridge University Press, 1997), and a valuable selection of Locke's *Writings on Religion* (ed. Victor Nuovo, Clarendon Press, 2002). Other published works of Locke are still most conveniently consulted in the 18th- or 19th-century editions of his *Collected Works*.

Maurice Cranston's *John Locke: A Biography* (Longman, London, 1957) is informative but less vivid than Laslett's Introduction to the *Two Treatises*. There is a major modern biography of Shaftesbury by K. H. D. Haley, *The First Earl of Shaftesbury* (Clarendon Press, Oxford, 1968), and a remarkable (if not invariably reliable) study of Locke's role in Shaftesbury's political enterprises in the late Richard Ashcraft's *Revolutionary Politics* and *Locke's Two Treatises of Government* (Princeton University Press, 1986). The Introductions by von Leyden and Abrams are particularly illuminating on the development of Locke's understanding of morality. The best systematic treatments of this are now provided by John Colman, *John Locke's Moral Philosophy* (Edinburgh University Press, 1983) and A. John Simmons, *The Lockean Theory of Rights* (Princeton University Press, 1992); but see also, more broadly, Ian Harris, *The Mind of John Locke* (Cambridge University Press, 1994). Locke's religious views are clearly (and on the whole approvingly) presented in M. S. Johnson, *Locke on Freedom* (Best Printing Co., Austin, Texas, 1978). They are also now widely discussed in studies of his political thinking (see, e.g., Dunn, 1969; Tully, 1980 and 1993; Marshall, 1994; Harris, 1994 below).

Michael Ayers's superb two-volume study *Locke. Epistemology and Ontology* (Routledge, 1991) stands head and shoulders above all other modern philosophical treatments of his philosophy as a whole. Amongst other helpful works, written from a wide variety of perspectives, are John W. Yolton, *Locke and the Compass of Human Understanding*

(Cambridge University Press, 1970); Roger Woolhouse, *Locke's Philosophy of Science and Knowledge* (Basil Blackwell, Oxford, 1971); Richard I. Aaron, *John Locke*, 3rd edn. (Clarendon Press, Oxford, 1971); James Gibson, *Locke's Theory of Knowledge and its Historical Relations* (Cambridge University Press, 1917); Kathleen Squadrito, *Locke's Theory of Sensitive Knowledge* (University Press of America, Washington, DC, 1978); J. L. Mackie, *Problems from Locke* (Clarendon Press, Oxford, 1976); Jonathan Bennett, *Locke, Berkeley, Hume: Central Themes* (Clarendon Press, Oxford, 1971) and *Learning from Six Philosophers*, 2 vols. (Oxford University Press, 2001), principally in Vol. 2; Peter A. Schouls, *The Imposition of Method* (Clarendon Press, Oxford, 1980); and the essays collected in I. C. Tipton (ed.), *Locke on Human Understanding* (Clarendon Press, Oxford, 1977). See now, too, Peter Schouls, *Reasoned Freedom: John Locke and Enlightenment* (Cornell University Press, 1992) and several of the chapters in Vere Chappell (ed.), *The Cambridge Companion to Locke* (Cambridge University Press, 1994). There are a number of important articles by Michael Ayers (see particularly 'Locke versus Aristotle on Natural Kinds', *Journal of Philosophy*, May 1981; ' Mechanism, Superaddition and the Proof of God's Existence in Locke's *Essay*', *Philosophical Review*, April 1981; 'The Ideas of Power and Substance in Locke's Philosophy', *Philosophical Quarterly*, January 1975). The central importance for Locke of men's responsibility for their own beliefs is brought out very elegantly in John Passmore, 'Locke and the Ethics of Belief', *Proceedings of the British Academy*, 1978. The relation between his conception of men's natural cognitive powers and the challenges with which History confronts them is discussed in J. Dunn, '"Bright Enough for all our Purposes": John Locke's Conception of a Civilised Society', *Notes and Records of the Royal Society*, 43 (1989). On his conception of education, see (in addition to the edition of J. W. and J. S. Yolton, 1989) Nathan Tarcov, *Locke's Education for Liberty* (University of Chicago Press, 1984). On Locke's conceptions of persons and their identity, see Ruth Mattern, 'Moral Science and the Concept of Persons in Locke', *Philosophical Review*, January 1980, and David Wiggins, 'Locke, Butler and the Stream of Consciousness and Men as a Natural Kind', in A. O. Rorty (ed.), *The Identities of Persons* (University of California Press, Berkeley,

1976). For the formation of Locke's own identity, see J. Dunn, 'Individuality and Clientage in the Formation of Locke's Social Imagination', in Reinhard Brandt (ed.), *John Locke* (W. de Gruyter, Berlin and New York, 1981). The originality and influence of Locke's conception of language is discussed magisterially in Hans Aarsleff, *From Locke to Saussure* (Athlone Press, London, 1982).

The best introductions to Locke's political thought are Geraint Parry, *Locke* (George Allen and Unwin, 1978) and Richard Ashcraft, *Locke's Two Treatises of Government* (George Allen and Unwin, 1987); but compare Ruth W. Grant, *John Locke's Liberalism* (University of Chicago Press, 1987). The *Two Treatises* itself is discussed in J. Dunn, *The Political Thought of John Locke* (Cambridge University Press, 1969). There are now also extremely valuable overall treatments of the *Two Treatises* in A. John Simmons, *The Lockean Theory of Rights* and *On the Edge of Anarchy* (Princeton University Press, 1992). Its analysis of property is best treated in James Tully, *A Discourse of Property* (Cambridge University Press, 1980). But compare Tully's recent collection, *An Approach to Political Philosophy. Locke in Contexts* (Cambridge University Press, 1993), Jeremy Waldron's careful and forceful, *The Right to Private Property* (Clarendon Press, Oxford, 1988), C. B. Macpherson, *The Political Theory of Possessive Individualism* (Clarendon Press, Oxford, 1962), the Introduction to Istvan Hont and Michael Ignatieff (eds.), *Wealth and Virtue* (Cambridge University Press, 1983), and Matthew Kramer, *John Locke and the Origins of Private Property* (Cambridge University Press, 1997). Political obligation is discussed by W. von Leyden, *Hobbes and Locke* (Macmillan, London, 1981); compare J. Dunn, *Political Obligation in its Historical Context* (Cambridge University Press, 1980), chapter 3. On toleration see especially the essays by Dunn and Goldie in O. P. Grell, Jonathan Israel, and Nicholas Tyacke (eds.), *From Persecution to Toleration* (Clarendon Press, Oxford, 1991), and Alex Tuckness, 'Rethinking the Intolerant Locke', *American Journal of Political Science*, 46, 2002. Two major recent systematic studies of his work as a whole from a historical point of view are Ian Harris, *The Mind of John Locke* and John Marshall, *John Locke, Resistance, Religion and Responsibility* (Cambridge University

Press, 1994). Both authors (alongside John Milton and Victor Nuovo) also have extremely valuable essays in M. A. Stewart (ed.), *English Philosophy in the Age of Locke* (Clarendon Press, 2000). There are several helpful articles in J. W. Yolton (ed.), *John Locke. Problems and Perspectives* (Cambridge University Press, 1969); see especially Ashcraft and Aarsleff. The most penetrating discussion of the evolution of Locke's own political commitments is to be found in Ashcraft's study, *Revolutionary Politics* (Princeton University Press, 1986), in a number of studies by Mark Goldie, notably, 'John Locke and Anglican Royalism', *Political Studies*, March 1983, and in the Introduction to Laslett's edition of the *Two Treatises*. There is a thoughtful and politically alert analysis of Locke's understanding of the conditions for governmental legitimacy in Peter Josephson's, *The Great Art of Government: Locke's Use of Consent* (University of Kansas Press, 2002): compare Kirstie McClure, *Judging Rights: Lockean Politics and the Limits of Consent* (Cornell University Press, 1996). For the pressing issue of how far Locke succeeded or failed in doing justice to the formidably different practical predicaments and interests of women, see especially Carole Pateman, *The Sexual Contract* (Polity, 1988), and A. John Simmons, 'The Conjugal and the Political in Locke', *Locke Studies*, 1 (2001), responding to Ruth Sample's, 'Locke on Political Authority and Conjugal Authority', *The Locke Newsletter*, 31, 2000.

The writings of the main target of the *Two Treatises*, Sir Robert Filmer, are available in convenient modern editions by Peter Laslett (Basil Blackwell, Oxford, 1949) and Johann P. Somerville (Cambridge University Press, 1991). The distinctiveness of Filmer's views is best brought out in James Daly, *Sir Robert Filmer and English Political Thought* (University of Toronto Press, 1979). The background to his thinking can be approached through Gordon J. Schochet, *Patriarchalism in Political Thought* (Basil Blackwell, Oxford, 1975). The relations between the political theory of Locke and his 18th-century successors are discussed in J. Dunn, 'The Politics of Locke in England and America in the Eighteenth Century', *Political Obligation*, chapter 4, and 'From Applied Theology to Social Analysis: The break between John Locke and the Scottish Enlightenment', in Hont and

Ignatieff (eds.), *Wealth and Virtue*, in Stephen Dworetz's somewhat brash, *The Unvarnished Doctrine* (Duke University Press, 1990), and in Michael Zuckert's learned and intelligent *Natural Rights and the New Republicanism* (Princeton University Press, 1995). I have attempted to assess the varying longevity and weight of Locke's impact upon subsequent political thinking in 'What is Living and What is Dead in Locke's Political Thought', in Dunn, *Interpreting Political Responsibility* (Polity, 1990), 'The Contemporary Political Significance of John Locke's Conception of Civil Society', in Sudipta Kaviraj and Sunil Khilnani (eds.), *Civil Society: History and Possibilities* (Cambridge University Press, 2001), and 'Measuring Locke's Shadow', in *Locke's Letter on Toleration and Two Treatises of Government* (ed. Ian Shapiro, Yale University Press, 2003). There are important modern studies on Locke's political theory in French (notably those of Jean-Fabien Spitz), German, Japanese, and Italian. An annual periodical, *The Locke Newsletter* (up to 2000), now *Locke Studies*, published by Roland Hall, Department of Philosophy, University of York, provides regular information on current research into Locke's life and thought. Its first issue was an invaluable bibliography, since republished in a fuller form as Roland Hall and Roger Woolhouse, *Eighty Years of Locke Scholarship. A Bibliographical* Guide (Edinburgh University Press, 1983).

Six works which illuminate the background to important aspects of Locke's writings are Michael Hunter, *Science and Society in Restoration England* (Cambridge University Press, 1981); Quentin Skinner, *The Foundations of Modern Political Thought* (2 vols., Cambridge University Press, 1978); Richard Tuck, *Natural Rights Theories: Their Origins and Development* (Cambridge University Press, 1979); and *Philosophy and Government 1572–1651* (Cambridge University Press, 1993); John W. Yolton, *John Locke and the Way of Ideas* (Clarendon Press, Oxford, 1956); Richard H. Popkin, *The History* of *Scepticism from Erasmus to Spinoza* (University of California Press, Berkeley, 1979).

Index

Locke

Locke